# The Turn of the Screw:

# The Study Guide Edition

By Francis Gilbert

This edition first published in 2015 by FGI publishing:
www.francisgilbert.co.uk;
fgipublishing.com
Copyright © 2015 Francis Gilbert
FGI Publishing, London UK, sir@francisgilbert.co.uk
British Library Cataloguing-in-Publications Data
A catalogue record for this book is available from the British Library.

ISBN-13: 978-1519448217
ISBN-10: 151944821X

**Dedication**
To Arifa

**Acknowledgments**
First, huge thanks must go to my wife, Erica Wagner, for always supporting me with my writing and teaching. Second, I'm very grateful to all the students, teachers, lecturers and other lively people who have helped me write this book.
Also by Francis Gilbert:
*I'm A Teacher, Get Me Out Of Here* (2004)
*Teacher On The Run* (2005)
*Yob Nation* (2006)
*Parent Power* (2007)
*Working The System: How To Get The Very State Education For Your Child* (2011)
*The Last Day Of Term* (2012)
Gilbert's Study Guides on: *Frankenstein, Far From The Madding Crowd, The Hound of the Baskervilles, Pride and Prejudice, The Strange Case of Dr Jekyll and Mr Hyde, The Turn of the Screw, Wuthering Heights* (2013)
*Dr Jekyll & Mr Hyde: The Study Guide Edition* (2014)
*Romeo and Juliet: The Study Guide Edition* (2014)
*Charlotte Brontë's Jane Eyre: The Study Guide Edition* (2015)
*Austen's Pride and Prejudice: The Study Guide Edition* (2015)
*Mary Shelley's Frankenstein: The Study Guide Edition* (2015)

# Contents

**INTRODUCTION** ........................................................6

**CONTEXTS** ............................................................6

UNDERSTANDING CONTEXTS ........................................ 6
CONTEXTS OF WRITING: HENRY JAMES'S LIFE ...................... 8
CONTEXTS OF READING .......................................... 11

**STRUCTURE AND THEME** ............................................ 14

**OPENING** ............................................................ 14

**COMPLICATIONS** .................................................. 15

**CRISIS** ............................................................ 15

**CLIMAX** ............................................................ 15

**RESOLUTION** ...................................................... 15

**THE INFLUENCE OF GENRE** ........................................ 17

THE ROLE OF THE GOTHIC .......................................17

**CRITICAL PERSPECTIVES** .......................................... 19

**PART 2: COMPLETE TEXT & TASKS** .............................. 21

HOW TO READ AND STUDY THE NOVEL ............................21

**THE TURN OF THE SCREW** ........................................ 23

PROLOGUE ...................................................... 23
*Questions* ....................................................*28*
CHAPTER 1 ...................................................... 29
*Questions* ....................................................*32*
CHAPTER 2 ...................................................... 33
*Questions* ....................................................*37*
CHAPTER 3 ...................................................... 37
*Questions* ....................................................*41*
CHAPTER 4 ...................................................... 41
*Questions* ....................................................*45*
CHAPTER 5 ...................................................... 45
*Questions* ....................................................*49*
CHAPTER 6 ...................................................... 49

*Questions* ............................................................................. *55*
CHAPTER 7 ............................................................................ *55*
*Questions* ............................................................................. *59*
CHAPTER 8 ............................................................................ *59*
*Questions* ............................................................................. *63*
CHAPTER 9 ............................................................................ *63*
*Questions* ............................................................................. *67*
CHAPTER 10 ........................................................................... *67*
*Questions* ............................................................................. *71*
CHAPTER 11 ........................................................................... *71*
*Questions* ............................................................................. *74*
CHAPTER 12 ........................................................................... *74*
*Questions* ............................................................................. *76*
CHAPTER 13 ........................................................................... *77*
*Questions* ............................................................................. *80*
CHAPTER 14 ........................................................................... *81*
*Questions* ............................................................................. *84*
CHAPTER 15 ........................................................................... *84*
*Questions* ............................................................................. *87*
CHAPTER 16 ........................................................................... *87*
*Questions* ............................................................................. *89*
CHAPTER 17 ........................................................................... *89*
*Questions* ............................................................................. *93*
CHAPTER 18 ........................................................................... *93*
*Questions* ............................................................................. *95*
CHAPTER 19 ........................................................................... *96*
*Questions* ............................................................................. *98*
CHAPTER 20 ........................................................................... *99*
*Questions* ............................................................................. *102*
CHAPTER 21 ........................................................................... *103*
*Questions* ............................................................................. *107*
CHAPTER 22 ........................................................................... *107*
*Questions* ............................................................................. *110*
CHAPTER 23 ........................................................................... *110*
*Questions* ............................................................................. *113*
CHAPTER 24 ........................................................................... *113*
*Questions* ............................................................................. *118*

**ANSWERS TO THE QUESTIONS** ............................................ **118**

*Prologue* ............................................................................. *119*
*Chapter 1* ........................................................................... *119*
*Chapter 2* ........................................................................... *119*
*Chapter 3* ........................................................................... *120*
*Chapter 4* ........................................................................... *120*
*Chapter 5* ........................................................................... *120*
*Chapter 6* ........................................................................... *120*
*Chapter 7* ........................................................................... *121*

*Chapter 8* .................................................................... *121*
*Chapter 9* .................................................................... *121*
*Chapter 10* .................................................................. *121*
*Chapter 11* ..................................................................*122*
*Chapter 12* ..................................................................*122*
*Chapter 13* ..................................................................*122*
*Chapter 14* ..................................................................*123*
*Chapter 15* ..................................................................*123*
*Chapter 16* ..................................................................*123*
*Chapter 17* ..................................................................*123*
*Chapter 18* ..................................................................*124*
*Chapter 19* ..................................................................*124*
*Chapter 20* .................................................................*124*
*Chapter 21* ..................................................................*125*
*Chapter 22* .................................................................*125*
*Chapter 23* .................................................................*125*
*Chapter 24* .................................................................*125*

**SPEAKING AND LISTENING EXERCISES**............................ **126**

**HOW TO WRITE TOP GRADE ESSAYS ON THE NOVEL** .......**127**

**POSSIBLE ESSAY TITLES** ................................................... **130**

**GLOSSARY** ...........................................................................**131**

**ABOUT THE AUTHOR**........................................................ **132**

# Introduction

This study guide takes a different approach from most study guides. It does not seek to tell you about the story and characters in a boring, useless fashion, but attempts to show how it is the author's techniques and interests that inform every single facet of this classic novel. Most study guides simply tell you *what* is going on, and tack on bits at the end which tell you *how* the writer created suspense and drama at certain points in the book, informing you a little about *why* the writer might have done this.

This study guide starts with the *how* and the *why*, showing you right from the start *how* and *why* the writer shaped the key elements of the book.

### Definition:

The context of a book is both the *world* the book creates in the reader's mind (contexts of reading), and the *world* it came out from (contexts of writing).

## How to use this Study Guide Edition

This study guide is deliberately interactive; it is full of questions, tasks and links to other sources of information. You will learn about *The Turn of the Screw* much more effectively if you have a go at the questions and tasks set, rather than just copying out notes.

# Contexts

## Understanding Contexts

In order to fully appreciate a text, you need to appreciate the contexts in which it was written – known as its contexts of writing – and the contexts in which you read the book, or the contexts of reading.

This is potentially a huge area to explore because 'contexts' essentially means the 'worlds' from which the book has arisen. For the best books, these are many and various. The most obvious starting point is the writer's own life: it is worth thinking about how and why the events in a writer's life might have influenced his or her fiction. However, you do have to be careful not to assume too much. For example, although the central character in the novel, the governess, bears some resemblance to Henry James' dead friend Minny Temple and his sister Alice, you must remember that the governess is a character in her own right in the novel – a vital cog in the narrative wheel, a literary construct and not a real person!

As a result, it is particularly fruitful to explore other contexts of writing. We can look at the broader world from which Henry James arose (Victorian, American and European culture), and consider carefully how, in his writing, he both adopted and rejected the morals of his time. Other contexts might be the influence of the literary world that Henry James inhabited (what other authors were writing at the time), how religion shaped his views, and so on.

Just as important as the contexts of *writing* are the contexts of *reading*: how we read the novel today. Central to this novel is whether we believe in ghosts or not: this novel leaves room for the reader to doubt whether the ghosts exist. Your own personal context is very important too. If you strongly believe in ghosts, then you will read this novel very differently from someone who does not. In order for you to fully consider the contexts of reading rather than my telling you what to think, I have posed open-ended questions that seem to me to be important when considering this issue.

# Questions

What do we mean by context? Why do you need to understand the idea of context in order to write well about *The Turn of the Screw*?

# Useful links

This BBC Bitesize webpage refers to poetry, but is relevant for all literature, providing a good visual organizer of the relevant things to think about when talking about context:
**http://www.bbc.co.uk/education/guides/z8kyg82/revision**

# Contexts of Writing: Henry James's Life

Henry James was the second son of the independently wealthy Henry and Mary James, and was born on 15ᵗʰ April, 1843 at 21 Washington Place, New York City. His brother, the first son, William had been born the year before. Almost immediately, his restless and intellectual father Henry James Senior, set about travelling to give his children the best education possible. The family visited Europe, staying in France and England, but returned to the US in 1845 to stay in Albany in New York State. Later, after the birth of two more sons, they moved to New York City, where Alice was born in 1848. This was perhaps the most settled period of Henry James' childhood, with the family staying in New York for seven years. In 1855, they were off on their travels again with Henry James Snr becoming obsessed with giving his children the best possible: they stayed in England, France and Switzerland, having a secession of private tutors. In 1858, they returned to America with the family taking up residence in Newport, Rhode Island. But in 1859, the family were back in Europe with Henry attending schools in Geneva and Bonn. In 1860, they returned to Newport. Henry and his fiercely intelligent brother William studied art: Henry was a very poor artist but the training gave him an interest in visual design and layout which would subsequently influence his writing a great deal. At this time, he was also writing poems and translating French authors.

In 1861, disaster nearly struck when Henry was injured while helping to put out a fire, an event which he would describe as "a horrid and obscure hurt". Meanwhile his brothers Wilky and Robertson fought on the Union side in the Civil War with William attending Lawrence Scientific School at Harvard. Feeling a failure at art, Henry attended a year at Harvard Law school; another venture which failed to bring him much success. In 1864, with the family uprooting to Boston and William attending Harvard Medical School, Henry began to forge a literary career: his first short story was published anonymously in the *Continental Monthly*. More success followed in 1865, with James publishing in his own name in the *Atlantic Monthly*. From 1866-68, the family moved yet again to Cambridge Massachusetts. Henry lived at home and continued writing, but in 1869 he went to Europe, travelling in England, France, Switzerland and Italy. In 1870, he learned of the death of his cousin Minny Temple, with whom he was very close: it appears that Minny was the model for many of his heroines. She was a highly intense, thoughtful woman who appears to have been as neurotic as the governess in *The Turn of the Screw*. He returned to the US where his first novel was published, but after that he was on his travels again, writing travel articles about his voyages in Europe.

By now James was becoming increasingly successful as a writer. He decided to settle in the cultural capital of the world then: Paris. He was appointed correspondent for the *New York Tribune*: a prestigious position. To add to his success, his new novel *Roderick Hudson* was published to favourable reviews. It was the beginning of a wonderful time for James: he met the great writers of the era and hobnobbed with the great and the good in England and in France, many of whom became personal friends. The great realist writers of the 19th century such as Turgenev, Flaubert and Zola were all close acquaintances to James. In December 1876, he moved to London, taking rooms in Bolton Street, Piccadilly. His life in Europe was full of industry and socialising. In 1881, he published his most famous novels, *Washington Square* and *The Portrait of a Lady*. Returning to the States in 1882, he continued working but both his parents died within a short space of each other. The following year he returned to England, continuing writing as well as trying to care for his demanding, sick sister, Alice. In 1885, he moved Alice to Bournemouth where the stricken Robert Louis Stevenson was staying. The two writers quickly became friends; it was friendship that was to prove fruitful for James, because, as we will see, he was influenced by Stevenson's ability to breathe new life into the tired genre of the Gothic.

From the mid-1880s, he continued working on some very ambitious projects: long novels, criticism, travel writing and short stories, but James did not replicate his early success at this point. To make matters worse, his sister died in 1892 and in 1895, his play *Guy Domville* was produced in London and was an unmitigated disaster. The criticism and fall-out from this disaster caused James to leave London: he was terribly wounded by the criticism he received. After the failure, he wrote in the form of a dialogue with himself: "I have my head, thank God, full of visions. One has never too many – one has never enough. Ah, just to let one's self go – at last: to surrender one's self to what through the long years one has (quite ironically, I think) hoped for and waited for..."

The comment upon having visions does not mean he literally had visions, but it is a telling comment nevertheless. His response to this crisis was to have 'waking visions', powerful ideas generated by the imagination. He was aware of his imagination and its power, but it seems that he clearly was interested in writing about someone who was not as knowing as himself, who had suffered a traumatic event, and who had visions. His most immediate response to the disaster of the play was that he moved to Lamb House, Rye in Sussex. It was there, still thinking about the idea of visions, he wrote *The Turn of the Screw*.

The story has its origin in a ghost-story which was recounted by the Archbishop of Canterbury at a country-house. We now have James' notebook which tells us how he sketched out the story. The notebook reveals that James had many of the elements in place before he wrote the story: the idea of the children being in the care of servants who die in very strange and mysterious circumstances and then reappear very dramatically. This point is perhaps what lies at much of the controversy of the story; some people do not believe the story is a ghost story, despite the fact that James called it one. Some critics believe it is a psychological tale, with the ghosts being hallucinations generated by the unbalanced governess. James wrote in his notebook: "It is all obscure and imperfect, the picture, the story, but there a suggestion of strangely gruesome effect in it. The tale to be told – tolerably obviously – by an outside spectator, an observer."

This is where he stays as he began to develop his fiction still further, pushing the boundaries of the novel at the time. In 1902, he published *The Wings of the Dove*, the first of his major great novels. This is followed by *The Ambassadors* (1903) and *The Golden Bowl* (1904). These three novels are generally regarded to be the first 'modernist' novels: they are very experimental. James used a 'stream-of-consciousness' style in them, mimicking the thought-processes of the human brain, revealing his characters to be sophisticated, shy, elusive thinkers. While James never attained the success of his early years, as he grew older, his position as a great man of literature became more secure. In 1915, he was naturalised as a British subject, after which he suffered from a stroke, from his never properly recovered. Nevertheless, he was well enough to accept the Order of Merit by King George V on New Year's Day of 1916. He died on 28th February of that year.

# Questions

Why do you think the book might be called *The Turn of the Screw*?
Clue: **http://www.shmoop.com/turn-of-the-screw/title.html**
What events, people and ideas in James's life and the wider society may have influenced the writing of the story?

# Useful links

This website devoted to Henry James is quirky and personalized, but contains a wealth of useful information:
**http://www.henryjames.org.uk/**
This website is full of academic links and definitely worth a browse:
**http://www2.newpaltz.edu/~hathaway/**
The Centre for Henry James Studies contains his letters and many other useful resources:
**http://centerforhenryjamesstudies.weebly.com/**
You can find detailed biographies here:
**http://www.online-literature.com/henry_james/**
**https://en.wikipedia.org/wiki/Henry_James**
There are good links for other websites here:
**http://www.webenglishteacher.com/henry-james.html**

# Selected Reading on Henry James's Life

Harry T. Moore: *Henry James and his world* (Thames and Hudson; 1974)

A marvellously readable, concise and fascinating biography of Henry James, complete with some fascinating photographs and pictures which really illuminate the world James came from.

Leon Edel: *Henry James – A Life* (Harper Collins; 1987)

This is the definitive biography of James. Edel spent twenty years writing his biography of James and published it in 5 volumes. This is the one volume version: much condensed for the general reader but nevertheless hugely readable.

# Contexts of Reading

We read this story very differently now than we did. During Henry James' time, there were serious scientists who believed that ghosts did exist: in the late nineteenth century, much of the Western world was in the grip of a mania connected with ghosts in a fashion which we just can't appreciate now. Respectable middle-class people, royalty, working class labourers would all do things like go to séances, where the dead would be called back, or attend spiritualist meetings which aimed to help the congregation to speak to the dead. Henry James, Sr., and William James were both members of the Society for Psychical Research, and William served as its president from 1894 to 1896, indicating that James' own family, intellectual and scientific as they were, clearly had a profound interest in the existence of spiritual phenomena.

Now, while there are many people who still do such things, they simply do not have the mainstream appeal or credibility that they had during the time when the short story was written. More likely than not, people believed in ghosts. This was a society which was profoundly superstitious and fearful: the Victorians developed their cemeteries in response to their fears about ghosts wandering the earth, not having been buried correctly.

Therefore, it is perhaps no surprise that when people first read James' story that they automatically assumed the ghosts were real: there was no debate about it. It was only over thirty years after the story was written, many years after James was dead, that the critic Edmund Wilson, influenced by the ideas of Freud, put forward the theory that the ghosts were products of the governess's imagination. By this time, society had changed: having experienced the industrialised death of the First World War, people were more sceptical about the supernatural and more inclined to see the 'evil' in human nature. Freud's theory that repressing sexual feelings, and childhood trauma could lead to people becoming 'neurotic' – mentally crippled by feelings of anxiety – was very fashionable by the time Wilson was writing in the 1920s. Wilson persuasively argued that the governess exhibited signs of neurosis in the way she responded so wildly to the children – hugging them one minute and chastising them the next. The underlying theme of sexual intrigue was clearly magnetic for many artists as well as critics. Benjamin Britten wrote an opera based on the short story which is perhaps the creepiest opera ever written. In the opera, there was great play made with some of the central ideas in the novel: that of silence, of control, of corruption. Most scarily, there is a sense that Quint has sexually abused Miles, and that the governess has an unnatural interest in the children as well. As is the case in the story, it's only hinted at, but it's more explicitly indicated than in James' story.

Perhaps the best ghost film ever made, *The Innocents* (1961), directed by Jack Clayton and starring Deborah Kerr, is a version of James' novel which develops and refines the themes of corruption and neurosis, traits very visible in the novel. The novel shares with the film some very powerful and stark visual imagery, but also a sense that the children are both innocent and corrupt, that they are clearly misunderstood by the adult world. In such a way, Clayton manages to bring to bear many of the fears that people in the 1960s had: that children are losing their way, being corrupted by the adult world, and that we don't know what to do about it, that all our meddling makes things worse, indeed corrupts even further. Inspired by the success of this low-budget money, many film-makers have attempted to film the story, with varying degrees of success. However, Britten's opera and Clayton's spooky black and white movie remain, despite the many other versions, the definite interpretations – and our well worth seeing.

The novel's obsession with children is what makes it especially spooky for us today. Even more so than the Victorians, we believe that childhood should be a sacrosanct place, a time of innocence and wonder, of love and imaginative play. However, we are all too aware that our children grow up too quickly, and are corrupted by the adult world that we inhabit and are entranced by. Miles and Flora with their precocious abilities and talk, their knowledge of the adult world, their friendship with the corrupt, debased Quint and Miss Jessel have become metaphors for modern children: old before their time, knowing and aware in a way that they shouldn't be. And yet, wearing the veneer of being perfect. Like many children today, they are neglected, fobbed off by paid employees rather than enjoying real familial love. Like the governess in the story, we try to interfere, to love and lead in the right direction, but the trouble is we are not aware of the right direction to go in. The fact that we have all these worries and concerns about children makes the novel even more resonant for us.

# Questions

It is worth doing some work on contexts before starting the actual book. I would suggest you write a *Turn of the Screw* **learning journal** that records all your thoughts and feelings about the book. Records the truth! After reading the book once, we will then look at academic responses but on the first reading we will really focus upon your thoughts about it.

There are two major questions to consider when thinking about contexts:

where is the book coming from and where am I coming from?

The first question is best answered while reading the book; what sorts of values and ideas are enshrined in this book? What is its historical context? What is its literary context? What is its philosophical context? How does the book relate to the life of the author?

It is worth you trying to analyse where you are coming from. Everyone holds a set of assumptions and ideas that profoundly affects how he or she sees the world. Try and answer these questions:

What are your attitudes towards adult and child relationships?

What are your attitudes towards ghosts? Do you believe they are real?

What is does innocence mean to you? Do you think innocent people can be corrupted? If so, how and why? If not, why?

# Useful links

The Wikipedia page on the book contains an informative section on all the adaptations of the film:

**https://en.wikipedia.org/wiki/The_Turn_of_the_Screw**

This YouTube video contains four different filmed versions of Quint at the window which is very useful to think about when considering how the story has been adapted:

**https://www.youtube.com/watch?v=X0LtqWZo2kg**

This webpage on the most successful version of the story on film, The Innocents, is insightful and detailed:

**http://moria.co.nz/horror/innocents-1961.htm**

The prize-winning novelist, Colm Toibin, writes very well about the story and *The Innocents* here:

**http://www.theguardian.com/books/2006/jun/03/fiction.colmtoibin**

There is a good webpage on filmed version on the BBC website here:

**http://www.bbcamerica.com/anglophenia/2013/10/forever-haunting-the-turn-of-the-screw-scares-again-and-again/**

## *Now onto the text*

What are the vital ingredients of a story? Why is that we are able to believe that a "whole load of words" contain a new world?

Now jot down your expectations about *The Turn of the Screw*. What kind of book do you expect it to be?

Write out what you think the story will be. Write out how you think it will be structured. What will be the main events of the story? Who will be the main characters?

While reading the novel, look back over the notes you have made for this section and constantly ask yourself; how does my context affect the way I read the novel and feel/think about the characters/situations/themes? I have already suggested that you write a learning journal as you read it through, jotting down these thoughts as you go along. Then once you have finished reading, think about the novel's overall effects and how it speaks to you personally.

Why do you think *The Turning of the Screw* is such a popular novel today? Why have so many films/plays/operas etc. been made of it?

# Structure and Theme

The novel is divided into twenty four short chapters which successively build up to the climatic point of Miles' death. The novel's central theme is that corruption: it explores it in many ways. Firstly, there is the obvious way in which the governess believes the ghosts are corrupting the children in the novel, leading them to think and do things that they shouldn't have. She believes that Miles was expelled from school because she was in some way corrupted by Peter Quint into lying, deceiving, stealing. We never learn what Miles actually did, so this is always open to interpretation. Most particularly, there is a sense that the governess believes that Quint and Miss Jessel were sexually corrupt, conducting an illicit affair, and inducting the children into their ways of sexual licentiousness. This is perhaps the most horrible aspect of the novel: we never quite know what the governess imagines the ghosts did, and so our own imaginations are left free to roam our deepest, darkest fears about adults with children. We could also say that the novel charts the corruption of the governess: she begins the novel with an honest intention to educate the children as best she can – but she ends it by effectively killing a child in her own care. We could say, if the ghosts were indeed figments of her own imagination, she was corrupted by her own fears and paranoia: she becomes progressively more controlling and paranoid during the novel, provoking Miles to an outburst which leads to him having a heart-attack. Moreover, she appears to draw Mrs Grose the housekeeper into her obsession, corrupting her in the process into providing details that prop up her own extreme notions that there are ghosts in the house. Thus we could say that the novel is about corruption on many levels: the corruption of adults, the corruption of children – and perhaps the corruption of the reader. We, ourselves, are left profoundly disturbed by the end of the novel because there is so much open-ended about the narrative: we never know for certain that there are ghosts, we never know whether Miles and Flora were abused, we never know what the governess's state of mind was. Our minds become corrupted by the same paranoia that infects the governess.

We could break down the novel into the following structure:

**Opening**

Introductory chapter, people telling ghost stories around the fireplace on Christmas Eve, a guest introduces a story about Flora and Miles told by a governess, with whom the guest was in love

We start reading the governess's written account. A handsome bachelor employs her to educate his nephew and niece at a country house in Essex after the governess has died.

## Complications

The governess meets Mrs Grose, a maid, and Flora, learning that Miles has been expelled from school. We never learn why. She sees a strange man on the tower of the house and, later, at the window of the dining-room, where she rushes to find him only to find he is gone, startling Mrs Grose in the process. Mrs Grose identifies the man as Peter Quint.

The governess becomes very watchful with Miles, worried that Quint is a malign influence upon the boy. One day, at a lake with Flora, she sees a woman in black: she believes Flora can see the ghost too but won't admit it. She works out, after a conversation with Mrs Grose, that the woman is Miss Jessel, the former governess.

## Crisis

The governess sees Quint on the stairs one night and Flora out of her bed, hiding behind some curtains. Flora won't say what she is doing. A few nights later, she sees Miss Jessel at the bottom of the stairs

Later on, she is awoken at midnight and finds Flora by the window, and discovers Miles is standing on the lawn.

The governess feels that Miles and Flora meet the ghosts a great deal and they are being corrupted by them. Mrs Grose asks her to write to their uncle, but the governess refuses, saying she'll leave if Mrs Grose writes to him.

## Climax

One Sunday, walking to church, Miles asks to go back to school, saying he will force his uncle to come to Bly. The governess is shocked and doesn't go to church, returning home and considering leaving altogether, when she sees Miss Jessel again. She shouts at Miss Jessel who disappears. She decides not to leave because she must protect the children. She agrees to write to the uncle.

Later, she and Mrs Grose find Flora by the lake, when the governess sees Miss Jessel again. Pointing the ghost out to Flora and Mrs Grose, they both say that they can see it. Flora says the governess is cruel. The governess breakdowns in hysterics.

## Resolution

Mrs Grose and the governess discover that the letter to the uncle was not sent because the servant, Luke, could not find it.

Flora becomes sick and leaves with Mrs Grose to go to the uncle to recover, leaving the governess with Miles.

The governess interrogates Miles, who admits to taking the letter. The governess screams when she sees Quint at the window, pointing him out to Miles, who asks if it is Quint but appears to see nothing. Clearly deeply traumatised by his interrogation and his possible sighting of the ghost, he dies from a heart attack.

# Useful links to help you get to know the novel better

The following websites are useful because they can give you a strong overview of the novel, but you really do need to think for yourself regarding your opinions of the novel.

http://www.sparknotes.com/lit/screw/summary.html
http://www.cliffsnotes.com/literature/t/the-turn-of-the-screw/book-summary
http://www.shmoop.com/turn-of-the-screw/summary.html
https://en.wikipedia.org/wiki/The_Turn_of_the_Screw
http://www.litcharts.com/lit/the-turn-of-the-screw/plot-overview
http://www.gradesaver.com/turn-of-the-screw/study-guide/summary
http://study.com/academy/lesson/the-turn-of-the-screw-by-henry-james-summary-characters-themes-analysis.html

The webpages contain quizzes which will test your knowledge.
http://www.cliffsnotes.com/literature/t/the-turn-of-the-screw/study-help/quiz
http://www.sparknotes.com/lit/screw/quiz.html
http://www.gradesaver.com/turn-of-the-screw/study-guide/quiz1
http://www.shmoop.com/turn-of-the-screw/quizzes.html

If you are **really struggling**, Penguin Readers has produced an abridged, "simple" version of the novel which can be found on PDF here:
https://docs.google.com/file/d/0BwTWaBxDgwkEaod4YWZLRm50MTA/edit?pli=1
There are teaching resources for this version here:
http://www.penguinreaders.com/pdf/downloads/pr/teachers-notes/9781405882057.pdf
http://www.penguinreaders.com/pdf/downloads/pr/activity-worksheets/9781405882057.pdf

# Questions/tasks

Once you have read the book, ask yourself this question: to what extent is the novel a successful story? What are its exciting moments and why? Are there moments when the story feels less successful? Give reasons for your answers.

Compare one or two filmed versions with the novel; what events/characters/ideas do the film-makers use and what do they leave out, and why?

# The Influence of Genre

## The Role of the Gothic

It was not that I didn't wait, on this occasion, for more, for I was
rooted as deeply as I was shaken.

Was there a "secret" at Bly--a mystery of Udolpho or an insane, an
unmentionable relative kept in unsuspected confinement? I can't say
how long I turned it over, or how long, in a confusion of curiosity and
dread, I remained where I had had my collision; I only recall that
when I re-entered the house darkness had quite closed in.

Early on in the novel, the governess speculates about whether Bly is like the
setting you might find in a Gothic novel. She refers to the famous fictional
setting of Udolpho. This was a setting in Ann Radcliffe's best-selling novel,
*The Mysteries of Udolpho* (1794). For many critics, this novel is the very
essence of the Gothic novel. It has all the key ingredients: haunting, ancient
castles and mansions, apparently ghostly events, a nasty, wicked villain and
a heroine who is persecuted for being good. The novel focuses upon Emily
St. Aubert, a French orphan who is imprisoned in the castle of Udolpho by
the villainous Signor Montoni. The plot is sensational, full of hysteria and
action, with undertones of racier content: sexual intrigue, murder,
corruption. It is fascinating that the governess mentions it because it was
much imitated and much mocked by the time Henry James came to write
his novel, nearly a hundred years later. Most famously, Jane Austen in her
novel, *Northanger Abbey*, parodied the novel by having a heroine who was
obsessed with the novel, so obsessed indeed that she jumped to all sorts of
false conclusions about the crumbling venue she was staying in. Austen
mocked the genre in this novel, making it clear that she thought it was far
too sensational and encouraged all sorts of hysterical thoughts. Her
underlying point was that the Gothic genre as a whole fostered diseased
minds: it encouraged wilful and wild speculation, and induced paranoia
and suspicion.

There is a sense in which one could read *The Turn of the Screw* as
making the same point. Much of the novel seems to follow the conventions
of the Gothic novel: there is a remote, crumbling setting, spooky nights, an
overwhelming sense of isolation, damsel in distress, the governess, and the
supernatural in the form of two wicked ghosts, Quint and Jessel -- as well
as an enigmatic owner of the house. However, unlike Austen's Northanger
Abbey, James' novel is far from being a comedy: it is overwhelmingly

serious in tone. That said, we can see that a possible interpretation of the book is that it is the governess' hysterical imagination which leads to the tragedy at the end. Thus we could say that James' point is almost identical to Austen's: people whose imaginations have been infected with nonsensical notions of the supernatural, notions that the Gothic genre deliberately tries to foster, are diseased and dangerous people. Certainly not people fit to hold a position of responsibility such as looking after children.

But the thing about James' writing is that one cannot categorise it so easily: Austen's point is crystal clear in *Northanger Abbey* – fevered imaginations are destructive – but James is far from so certain: there is always the sense that the governess may just be right. We are never certain that the ghosts don't exist. Indeed, James does not mock the conventions of the Gothic but pays homage to them, developing and refining them to make the genre live again. He takes a very well-worn formula of the haunted house and breathes new life into it by making the story intensely claustrophobic, and psychological in approach. There is no doubt that here a big influence was the writing of his friend Robert Louis Stevenson, whose *Strange Case Of Dr Jekyll and Mr Hyde*, also pushed the boundaries of the Gothic genre, taking it in a much more psychological realm.

In this sense, James' model was not primarily the Gothic but the social realist novels written by him and other nineteenth century writers like George Eliot, Turgenev, Emile Zola, Gustave Flaubert. These were all writers whose primary interest was in writing about the human character in a realistic and psychologically truthful fashion: describing thoughts, feelings, sensations, sights, sounds, smells, and tastes in a very vivid fashion so that the reader had a real sense of living inside the minds of their characters. Compared with most Gothic novels, very little actually happens in The Turn of the Screw. Indeed, apart from the death of Miles at the very end, it could be argued that virtually nothing happens at all except a few major events: Miles' expulsion from school and the disappearance of the letter. Other events such as Miles standing on the lawn at midnight and Flora hiding behind a curtain seem relatively trivial when looked at coldly. However, because James takes us so vividly into the mind of the governess, we feel that they are momentous events. It is the way that James' anatomizes the mind of the governess which gives the novel its lasting power: whether we believe in the ghosts or not, we are gripped by the realistic description of her changing thoughts, feelings and responses to the events around her..

# Questions for Genre

How was James influenced by other writers and genres in the writing of the story? Where did he get his ideas for his characters from?

## Useful links

http://www.newyorker.com/books/page-turner/ever-scarier-on-the-turn-of-the-screw

http://www.criminalelement.com/blogs/2014/09/the-turn-of-the-screw-a-gothic-whatdunit-henry-james-ghost-story-michael-nethercott

# Critical Perspectives

## How reliable is the narrator?

What do the hugely successful horror films *The Blair Witch Project* and *The Sixth Sense* have in common with the fiction of Henry James? Even if you are aware of these films, you'll probably say not much. After all, Henry James is famous for writing impenetrable, highly ornate novels about upper-crust Americans and Europeans who lived in the late Victorian times and his name is rarely associated with popular movies that star Bruce Willis.

However, Henry James is not the rarefied writer that many people think he is. *The Turn of the Screw* is one of the author's best stories and has many similarities with the chiller-thriller *The Sixth Sense*. Both narratives use children as their main characters and generate suspense by being disturbing, scary stories. While many people couldn't sleep after seeing the Hollywood movie, I think that James's story is more frightening. *The Sixth Sense* is about a disillusioned psychiatrist, played by Bruce Willis, who helps a young boy who is troubled by visions of dead people. James's story employs a similar narrative device of having children conversing with the dead. Moreover, what makes the boy terrifying in *The Sixth Sense* is what makes Miles terrifying in James' fiction: his inscrutability. We never quite know what the boy is up to until the very end of the movie. Ultimately, the film hinges upon the fact that the narrator of the movie, Bruce Willis, is unreliable: he doesn't know the full truth.

Henry James pioneered the technique of the unreliable narrator: in just the same way that *The Sixth Sense* is told exclusively from Bruce Willis's point of view, so too *The Turn of the Screw* is recounted from the sexually repressed governess's vantage point. James manages to make the reader sympathise with the teacher's plight but also see that the ghosts could be figments of her hysterical imagination. Real mystery is engendered because the reader never quite knows who is evil. Are the children really so two-faced that they are conspiring with two malevolent spooks or is the over-anxious but caring tutor losing her mind to paranoia? The unreliable narration of the governess is vital in creating this kind of suspense because if we believed her fully there would be very little mystery.

Henry James was intrigued by his experiences of both America and Europe. In many ways, all of his work – including *The Turn of the Screw* in a very oblique way -- explores the corrupt but sophisticated hypocrisy of Europeans and the effect they had on visiting Americans. Many of his novels start from the simple premise of a wealthy American journeying around Europe and finding him or herself embroiled with a seductive, older European man or woman who is usually after the American's money or seeking to shatter their peace of mind. Of course this is a crude generalisation because James's work is very subtle: he observes the tiniest changes of emotions and the smallest shifts in power that occur between people as they get to know each other. This is what makes James's novels so exciting. Human relations are like a poker game where the highest stakes are being played for. While *The Turn of the Screw* does not have any American characters in it, it is not difficult to see that the governess is rather like an American arriving in Europe in this novel: in much the same way James's American jump to conclusions about the world they see in Europe, the governess begins jumping to conclusions about the situation at Bly. Her suspicions, her fears, her paranoia are like the paranoia of a person in a very foreign land, but feel they understand it. She is an unreliable narrator because she feels so certain in the truth of what she sees: she has the brash assurance that James felt was characteristic of his countrymen.

# Selected Reading and weblinks on *The Turn of the Screw*

Peter G. Beidler (editor): *The Turn of the Screw – Case Studies in Contemporary Criticism* (Bedford/St. Martins; 2003)

This volume presents the text of the New York Edition of James's classic 1898 short novel along with critical essays that read *The Turn of the Screw* from contemporary reader-response, psychoanalytic, gender, and Marxist perspectives.

This website is a PhD thesis, but it is clearly written and nicely indexed:
**http://www.turnofthescrew.com/**
Other useful links are here:
**http://www.studentpulse.com/articles/65/literary-analysis-turn-of-the-screw**
**http://www.davidappleyard.com/scribbles/hjames.htm**

# Questions

What differing views do literary critics have of the novel? Which critics do you most agree with and why? Which ones do you agree with the least and why?

# Part 2: Complete text & tasks

## How to read and study the novel

What follows is the complete text of *The Turn of the Screw* interspersed with commentaries and questions on the text. The text is broken up with analysis and points for discussion. I have deliberately provided a variety of different question types at the ends of chapters; I have started with "simple" comprehension questions and then moved onto more analytical and creative questions, which not only require you to understand the plot but also arrive at your own personal responses, using evidence from the text to back up your points. The GCSE/A Level questions that follow the comprehension ones are more difficult and don't usually have "right and wrong" answers. The GCSE style questions are the sorts of questions you might typically get in a GCSE exam; the same is true for the A Level questions, which usually invite students to show they have read more and are able to compare and contrast texts in depth. Please interpret the categories of GCSE/A Level in a relaxed fashion: have a go at the exercises which will help you rather than rigidly sticking to the exercises that are "your level". The categories are only rough guidelines. I sometimes ask you to devise a visual organiser to represent ideas/characters/plot-lines in the novel; this means doing a spider-diagram/chart/flow diagram etc. depending upon what you feel is most relevant. To find out more (sometimes known as graphic organisers) look here:

**https://www.teachingenglish.org.uk/article/graphic-organisers**

Remember if you are uncertain about the plot, you can also refer to the websites listed in the section **'Useful links to help you get to know the story better'**. These websites are good at helping you understand the plot but they won't help you get the higher marks because you really need to think for yourself if you are going to get the top grades.

As I have suggested, you could, while reading the book, put all your answers, notes, creative responses together into a *Turn of the Screw* file or **learning journal**. You could be creative with this file: draw scenes of the important incidents; include spider-diagrams/visual organisers of significant characters and situations; storyboards of the key scenes; copies of articles/literary criticism which you have annotated; creative pieces etc.

# Helpful vocabulary to learn before you start reading

Throughout the book, **you should keep a vocabulary list**, writing down the difficult words and learning their meanings/spellings, and possibly using the vocabulary in your own writing. The complex vocabulary and sentence structures in the story can be off-putting at first but I feel you should not be put off by the language; embrace it, love it! You will become much better educated when you learn the vocabulary. This is why reading pre-20th century writing is so useful: it makes you more intelligent because you widen your vocabulary and ability to understand difficult passages.

There are some words, I would strongly advise you looking up the meanings of and learning their spellings/meanings before reading; the websites listed below are helpful in this regard.

# Weblinks to help you learn difficult vocabulary

The following websites are all quizzes on the difficult words in the book, which also provide the meanings of the words (after you have had a go at the quiz!). Remember though nothing beats looking up words for yourself!

**http://www.vocabulary.com/lists/283048#view=notes**
**https://quizlet.com/4903249/the-turn-of-the-screw-vocabulary-flash-cards/**
**http://www.verbalworkout.com/b/b1277.htm**
**http://www.proprofs.com/flashcards/story.php?title=vocabulary-turn--screw**

This is a sample of a study guide which contains some good vocabulary lists as well:
**https://www.prestwickhouse.com/samples/301162.pdf**

# The Turn of the Screw

Henry James

## Prologue

The story had held us, round the fire, sufficiently breathless, but except the obvious remark that it was gruesome, as, on Christmas Eve in an old house, a strange tale should essentially be, I remember no comment uttered till somebody happened to say that it was the only case he had met in which such a visitation had fallen on a child. The case, I may mention, was that of an apparition in just such an old house as had gathered us for the occasion—an appearance, of a dreadful kind, to a little boy sleeping in the room with his mother and waking her up in the terror of it; waking her not to dissipate his dread and soothe him to sleep again, but to encounter also, herself, before she had succeeded in doing so, the same sight that had shaken him. It was this observation that drew from Douglas—not immediately, but later in the evening—a reply that had the interesting consequence to which I call attention. Someone else told a story not particularly effective, which I saw he was not following. This I took for a sign that he had himself something to produce and that we should only have to wait. We waited in fact till two nights later; but that same evening, before we scattered, he brought out what was in his mind.

"I quite agree—in regard to Griffin's ghost, or whatever it was—that its appearing first to the little boy, at so tender an age, adds a particular touch. But it's not the first occurrence of its charming kind that I know to have involved a child. If the child gives the effect another turn of the screw, what do you say to TWO children—?"

"We say, of course," somebody exclaimed, "that they give two turns! Also that we want to hear about them."

I can see Douglas there before the fire, to which he had got up to present his back, looking down at his interlocutor with his hands in his pockets. "Nobody but me, till now, has ever heard. It's quite too horrible." This, naturally, was declared by several voices to give the thing the utmost price, and our friend, with quiet art, prepared his triumph by turning his eyes over the rest of us and going on: "It's beyond everything. Nothing at all that I know touches it."

"For sheer terror?" I remember asking.

He seemed to say it was not so simple as that; to be really at a loss how to qualify it. He passed his hand over his eyes, made a little wincing grimace. "For dreadful—dreadfulness!"

"Oh, how delicious!" cried one of the women.

He took no notice of her; he looked at me, but as if, instead of me, he saw what he spoke of. "For general uncanny ugliness and horror and pain."

"Well then," I said, "just sit right down and begin."

He turned round to the fire, gave a kick to a log, watched it an instant. Then as he faced us again: "I can't begin. I shall have to send to town." There was a unanimous groan at this, and much reproach; after which, in his preoccupied way, he explained. "The story's written. It's in a locked drawer—it has not been out for years. I could write to my man and enclose the key; he could send down the packet as he finds it." It was to me in particular that he appeared to propound this—appeared almost to appeal for aid not to hesitate. He had broken a thickness of ice, the formation of many a winter; had had his reasons for a long silence. The others resented postponement, but it was just his scruples that charmed me. I adjured him to write by the first post and to agree with us for an early hearing; then I asked him if the experience in question had been his own. To this his answer was prompt. "Oh, thank God, no!"

"And is the record yours? You took the thing down?"

"Nothing but the impression. I took that HERE"—he tapped his heart. "I've never lost it."

"Then your manuscript—?"

"Is in old, faded ink, and in the most beautiful hand." He hung fire again. "A woman's. She has been dead these twenty years. She sent me the pages in question before she died." They were all listening now, and of course there was somebody to be arch, or at any rate to draw the inference. But if he put the inference by without a smile it was also without irritation. "She was a most charming person, but she was ten years older than I. She was my sister's governess," he quietly said. "She was the most agreeable woman I've ever known in her position; she would have been worthy of any whatever. It was long ago, and this episode was long before.

## Analysis:
The novella opens with a description of a Christmas Eve at an ancient house where a group are listening to each other's ghost stories. The atmosphere is slightly spooky, but jolly as well. As an introduction to the main story of the evening, a person called Douglas tells about two children – Flora and Miles – and his sister's governess who he was in love with. This is a vital piece of information because it introduces the key theme of sexual desire, which is explored in some depth in a coded fashion during this story. Notice the language of attraction is hidden at this point: he simply describes the woman as "agreeable". Moreover, it makes us realise that the governess of the story is no plain frump, but a desirable woman.

## Discussion point:
Why does James start the story not with the main narrator but with a gathering where ghost stories are being told?

I was at Trinity, and I found her at home on my coming down the second summer. I was much there that year—it was a beautiful one; and we had, in her off-hours, some strolls and talks in the garden—talks in which she struck me as awfully clever and nice. Oh yes; don't grin: I liked her extremely and am glad to this day to think she liked me, too. If she hadn't she wouldn't have told me. She had never told anyone. It wasn't simply that she said so, but that I knew she hadn't. I was sure; I could see. You'll easily judge why when you hear."

"Because the thing had been such a scare?"

He continued to fix me. "You'll easily judge," he repeated: "YOU will."

I fixed him, too. "I see. She was in love."

He laughed for the first time. "You ARE acute. Yes, she was in love. That is, she had been. That came out—she couldn't tell her story without its coming out. I saw it, and she saw I saw it; but neither of us spoke of it. I remember the time and the place—the corner of the lawn, the shade of the great beeches and the long, hot summer afternoon. It wasn't a scene for a shudder; but oh—!" He quitted the fire and dropped back into his chair.

"You'll receive the packet Thursday morning?" I inquired.

"Probably not till the second post."

"Well then; after dinner—"

"You'll all meet me here?" He looked us round again. "Isn't anybody going?" It was almost the tone of hope.

"Everybody will stay!"

"I will"—and "I will!" cried the ladies whose departure had been fixed. Mrs. Griffin, however, expressed the need for a little more light. "Who was it she was in love with?"

"The story will tell," I took upon myself to reply.

"Oh, I can't wait for the story!"

"The story WON'T tell," said Douglas; "not in any literal, vulgar way."

"More's the pity, then. That's the only way I ever understand."

"Won't YOU tell, Douglas?" somebody else inquired.

He sprang to his feet again. "Yes—tomorrow. Now I must go to bed. Good night." And quickly catching up a candlestick, he left us slightly bewildered. From our end of the great brown hall we heard his step on the stair; whereupon Mrs. Griffin spoke. "Well, if I don't know who she was in love with, I know who HE was."

"She was ten years older," said her husband.

"Raison de plus—at that age! But it's rather nice, his long reticence."

"Forty years!" Griffin put in.

"With this outbreak at last."

"The outbreak," I returned, "will make a tremendous occasion of Thursday night;" and everyone so agreed with me that, in the light of it, we lost all attention for everything else. The last story, however incomplete and like the mere opening of a serial, had been told; we handshook and "candlestuck," as somebody said, and went to bed.

I knew the next day that a letter containing the key had, by the first post, gone off to his London apartments; but in spite of—or perhaps just on account of—the eventual diffusion of this knowledge we quite let him alone till after dinner, till such an hour of the evening, in fact, as might best accord with the kind of emotion on which our hopes were fixed. Then he became as communicative as we could desire and indeed gave us his best reason for being so. We had it from him again before the fire in the hall, as we had had our mild wonders of the previous night. It appeared that the narrative he had promised to read us really required for a proper intelligence a few words of prologue. Let me say here distinctly, to have done with it, that this narrative, from an exact transcript of my own made much later, is what I shall presently give. Poor Douglas, before his death—when it was in sight—committed to me the manuscript that reached him on the third of these days and that, on the same spot, with immense effect, he began to read to our hushed little circle on the night of the fourth. The departing ladies who had said they would stay didn't, of course, thank heaven, stay: they departed, in consequence of arrangements made, in a rage of curiosity, as they professed, produced by the touches with which he had already worked us up. But that only made his little final auditory more compact and select, kept it, round the hearth, subject to a common thrill.

The first of these touches conveyed that the written statement took up the tale at a point after it had, in a manner, begun. The fact to be in possession of was therefore that his old friend, the youngest of several daughters of a poor country parson, had, at the age of twenty, on taking service for the first time in the schoolroom, come up to London, in trepidation, to answer in person an advertisement that had already placed her in brief correspondence with the advertiser. This person proved, on her presenting herself, for judgment, at a house in Harley Street, that impressed her as vast and imposing—this prospective patron proved a gentleman, a bachelor in the prime of life, such a figure as had never risen, save in a dream or an old novel, before a fluttered, anxious girl out of a Hampshire vicarage. One could easily fix his type; it never, happily, dies out. He was handsome and bold and pleasant, offhand and gay and kind. He struck her, inevitably, as gallant and splendid, but what took her most of all and gave her the courage she afterward showed was that he put the whole thing to her as a kind of favor, an obligation he should gratefully incur. She conceived him as rich, but as fearfully extravagant—saw him all in a glow of high fashion, of good looks, of expensive habits, of charming ways with women. He had for his own town residence a big house filled with the spoils of travel and the trophies of the chase; but it was to his country home, an old family place in Essex, that he wished her immediately to proceed.

He had been left, by the death of their parents in India, guardian to a small nephew and a small niece, children of a younger, a military brother, whom he had lost two years before. These children were, by the strangest of chances for a man in his position—a lone man without the right sort of experience or a grain of patience—very heavily on his hands. It had all been a great worry and, on his own part doubtless, a series of blunders, but he immensely pitied the poor chicks and had done all he could; had in particular sent them down to his other house, the proper place for them being of course the country, and kept them there, from the first, with the best people he could find to look after them, parting even with his own servants to wait on them and going down himself, whenever he might, to see how they were doing. The awkward thing was that they had practically no other relations and that his own affairs took up all his time. He had put them in possession of Bly, which was healthy and secure, and had placed at the head of their little establishment—but below stairs only—an excellent woman, Mrs. Grose, whom he was sure his visitor would like and who had formerly been maid to his mother. She was now housekeeper and was also acting for the time as superintendent to the little girl, of whom, without children of her own, she was, by good luck, extremely fond.

Analysis: We are provided with some background to the story before it begins properly: we learn the governess was appointed by a handsome unmarried man to take care of his orphaned nephew and niece. Notice how the character of Mrs Grose is introduced as a character: she is of a lower class, a "maid", and a "superintendent" to Flora. However, she is "below stairs": Mrs Grose's lowly social position is very important in the story because it renders her powerless to deal with the growing hysteria of the governess towards the end of the story. The reader's assumption initially is that she is a simple woman because she is lower class, but we realise that this is not the case as the story progresses.

Discussion point: Why does James choose as his setting an old country house in Essex?

There were plenty of people to help, but of course the young lady who should go down as governess would be in supreme authority. She would also have, in holidays, to look after the small boy, who had been for a term at school—young as he was to be sent, but what else could be done?—and who, as the holidays were about to begin, would be back from one day to the other. There had been for the two children at first a young lady whom they had had the misfortune to lose. She had done for them quite beautifully—she was a most respectable person—till her death, the great awkwardness of which had, precisely, left no alternative but the school for little Miles. Mrs. Grose, since then, in the way of manners and things, had done as she could for Flora; and there were, further, a cook, a housemaid, a dairywoman, an old pony, an old groom, and an old gardener, all likewise thoroughly respectable.

So far had Douglas presented his picture when someone put a question. "And what did the former governess die of?—of so much respectability?"

Our friend's answer was prompt. "That will come out. I don't anticipate."

"Excuse me—I thought that was just what you ARE doing."

"In her successor's place," I suggested, "I should have wished to learn if the office brought with it—"

"Necessary danger to life?" Douglas completed my thought. "She did wish to learn, and she did learn. You shall hear tomorrow what she learned. Meanwhile, of course, the prospect struck her as slightly grim. She was young, untried, nervous: it was a vision of serious duties and little company, of really great loneliness. She hesitated—took a couple of days to consult and consider. But the salary offered much exceeded her modest measure, and on a second interview she faced the music, she engaged." And Douglas, with this, made a pause that, for the benefit of the company, moved me to throw in—

"The moral of which was of course the seduction exercised by the splendid young man. She succumbed to it."

He got up and, as he had done the night before, went to the fire, gave a stir to a log with his foot, then stood a moment with his back to us. "She saw him only twice."

"Yes, but that's just the beauty of her passion."

A little to my surprise, on this, Douglas turned round to me. "It WAS the beauty of it. There were others," he went on, "who hadn't succumbed. He told her frankly all his difficulty—that for several applicants the conditions had been prohibitive. They were, somehow, simply afraid. It sounded dull— it sounded strange; and all the more so because of his main condition."

"Which was—?"

"That she should never trouble him—but never, never: neither appeal nor complain nor write about anything; only meet all questions herself, receive all moneys from his solicitor, take the whole thing over and let him alone. She promised to do this, and she mentioned to me that when, for a moment, disburdened, delighted, he held her hand, thanking her for the sacrifice, she already felt rewarded."

"But was that all her reward?" one of the ladies asked.

"She never saw him again."

"Oh!" said the lady; which, as our friend immediately left us again, was the only other word of importance contributed to the subject till, the next night, by the corner of the hearth, in the best chair, he opened the faded red cover of a thin old-fashioned gilt-edged album. The whole thing took indeed more nights than one, but on the first occasion the same lady put another question. "What is your title?"

"I haven't one."

"Oh, I have!" I said. But Douglas, without heeding me, had begun to read with a fine clearness that was like a rendering to the ear of the beauty of his author's hand.

## Questions

What do the guests at the house party think makes a creepy story?

What story does Douglas say he knows about?

What does Douglas need to do in order to tell the story?

What connection does Douglas have with the author of the story?

What does Douglas explain was the circumstances of the writing of the story? How old was the governess and why was she put in charge of two children?

On what condition must the governess take the work?

Why does the governess possibly accept the position?

GCSE style question: how effective is this Prologue as the beginning of the story? Why do you think James included a Prologue?

A Level style question: compare and contrast this Prologue with another Prologue in a story/play/poem. What are the similarities and differences?

Creative response: write a description of a group of people telling each other ghost stories; think carefully about the setting, the characters and why they are telling each other ghost stories.

You can find brief answers in the section, **Answers to the Questions**.

# Chapter 1

I remember the whole beginning as a succession of flights and drops, a little seesaw of the right throbs and the wrong. After rising, in town, to meet his appeal, I had at all events a couple of very bad days—found myself doubtful again, felt indeed sure I had made a mistake. In this state of mind I spent the long hours of bumping, swinging coach that carried me to the stopping place at which I was to be met by a vehicle from the house. This convenience, I was told, had been ordered, and I found, toward the close of the June afternoon, a commodious fly in waiting for me. Driving at that hour, on a lovely day, through a country to which the summer sweetness seemed to offer me a friendly welcome, my fortitude mounted afresh and, as we turned into the avenue, encountered a reprieve that was probably but a proof of the point to which it had sunk. I suppose I had expected, or had dreaded, something so melancholy that what greeted me was a good surprise. I remember as a most pleasant impression the broad, clear front, its open windows and fresh curtains and the pair of maids looking out; I remember the lawn and the bright flowers and the crunch of my wheels on the gravel and the clustered treetops over which the rooks circled and cawed in the golden sky. The scene had a greatness that made it a different affair from my own scant home, and there immediately appeared at the door, with a little girl in her hand, a civil person who dropped me as decent a curtsy as if I had been the mistress or a distinguished visitor. I had received in Harley Street a narrower notion of the place, and that, as I recalled it, made me think the proprietor still more of a gentleman, suggested that what I was to enjoy might be something beyond his promise.

I had no drop again till the next day, for I was carried triumphantly through the following hours by my introduction to the younger of my pupils. The little girl who accompanied Mrs. Grose appeared to me on the spot a creature so charming as to make it a great fortune to have to do with her. She was the most beautiful child I had ever seen, and I afterward wondered that my employer had not told me more of her. I slept little that night—I was too much excited; and this astonished me, too, I recollect, remained with me, adding to my sense of the liberality with which I was treated. The large, impressive room, one of the best in the house, the great state bed, as I almost felt it, the full, figured draperies, the long glasses in which, for the first time, I could see myself from head to foot, all struck me—like the extraordinary charm of my small charge—as so many things thrown in. It was thrown in as well, from the first moment, that I should get on with Mrs. Grose in a relation over which, on my way, in the coach, I fear I had rather brooded. The only thing indeed that in this early outlook might have made me shrink again was the clear circumstance of her being so glad to see me. I perceived within half an hour that she was so glad— stout, simple, plain, clean, wholesome woman—as to be positively on her guard against showing it too much. I wondered even then a little why she should wish not to show it, and that, with reflection, with suspicion, might of course have made me uneasy.

But it was a comfort that there could be no uneasiness in a connection with anything so beatific as the radiant image of my little girl, the vision of whose angelic beauty had probably more than anything else to do with the restlessness that, before morning, made me several times rise and wander about my room to take in the whole picture and prospect; to watch, from my open window, the faint summer dawn, to look at such portions of the rest of the house as I could catch, and to listen, while, in the fading dusk, the first birds began to twitter, for the possible recurrence of a sound or two, less natural and not without, but within, that I had fancied I heard. There had been a moment when I believed I recognized, faint and far, the cry of a child; there had been another when I found myself just consciously starting as at the passage, before my door, of a light footstep. But these fancies were not marked enough not to be thrown off, and it is only in the light, or the gloom, I should rather say, of other and subsequent matters that they now come back to me. To watch, teach, "form" little Flora would too evidently be the making of a happy and useful life. It had been agreed between us downstairs that after this first occasion I should have her as a matter of course at night, her small white bed being already arranged, to that end, in my room. What I had undertaken was the whole care of her, and she had remained, just this last time, with Mrs. Grose only as an effect of our consideration for my inevitable strangeness and her natural timidity. In spite of this timidity—which the child herself, in the oddest way in the world, had been perfectly frank and brave about, allowing it, without a sign of uncomfortable consciousness, with the deep, sweet serenity indeed of one of Raphael's holy infants, to be discussed, to be imputed to her, and to determine us—I feel quite sure she would presently like me. It was part of what I already liked Mrs. Grose herself for, the pleasure I could see her feel in my admiration and wonder as I sat at supper with four tall candles and with my pupil, in a high chair and a bib, brightly facing me, between them, over bread and milk. There were naturally things that in Flora's presence could pass between us only as prodigious and gratified looks, obscure and roundabout allusions.

"And the little boy—does he look like her? Is he too so very remarkable?"

One wouldn't flatter a child. "Oh, miss, MOST remarkable. If you think well of this one!"—and she stood there with a plate in her hand, beaming at our companion, who looked from one of us to the other with placid heavenly eyes that contained nothing to check us.

"Yes; if I do—?"

"You WILL be carried away by the little gentleman!"

"Well, that, I think, is what I came for—to be carried away. I'm afraid, however," I remember feeling the impulse to add, "I'm rather easily carried away. I was carried away in London!"

I can still see Mrs. Grose's broad face as she took this in. "In Harley Street?"

"In Harley Street."

"Well, miss, you're not the first—and you won't be the last."

"Oh, I've no pretension," I could laugh, "to being the only one. My other pupil, at any rate, as I understand, comes back tomorrow?"

"Not tomorrow—Friday, miss. He arrives, as you did, by the coach, under care of the guard, and is to be met by the same carriage."

I forthwith expressed that the proper as well as the pleasant and friendly thing would be therefore that on the arrival of the public conveyance I should be in waiting for him with his little sister; an idea in which Mrs. Grose concurred so heartily that I somehow took her manner as a kind of comforting pledge—never falsified, thank heaven!—that we should on every question be quite at one. Oh, she was glad I was there!

What I felt the next day was, I suppose, nothing that could be fairly called a reaction from the cheer of my arrival; it was probably at the most only a slight oppression produced by a fuller measure of the scale, as I walked round them, gazed up at them, took them in, of my new circumstances. They had, as it were, an extent and mass for which I had not been prepared and in the presence of which I found myself, freshly, a little scared as well as a little proud. Lessons, in this agitation, certainly suffered some delay; I reflected that my first duty was, by the gentlest arts I could contrive, to win the child into the sense of knowing me. I spent the day with her out-of-doors; I arranged with her, to her great satisfaction, that it should be she, she only, who might show me the place. She showed it step by step and room by room and secret by secret, with droll, delightful, childish talk about it and with the result, in half an hour, of our becoming immense friends.

> **Analysis:** We gain a real sense of the anxiety of the governess at the beginning of her narrative because she is so worried about getting on with her "charges" – her pupils. We realise though that the governess is a good and receptive teacher though, encouraging Flora to show her the house – to be in charge as it were. We also see how much the governess delights in the "childish" talk of Flora. The result of this is that they become "immense friends" – here we see the ambivalent feelings of the governess sneaking into her narrative. She is "childish" herself: she wants to be fantastic friends with Flora more than being the adult responsible for her.

> **Discussion point:** How important is it for teachers to become "immense friends" with their pupils? What are the advantages and disadvantages of becoming friends with one's pupils?

Young as she was, I was struck, throughout our little tour, with her confidence and courage with the way, in empty chambers and dull corridors, on crooked staircases that made me pause and even on the summit of an old machicolated square tower that made me dizzy, her morning music, her disposition to tell me so many more things than she asked, rang out and led me on. I have not seen Bly since the day I left it, and I daresay that to my older and more informed eyes it would now appear sufficiently contracted. But as my little conductress, with her hair of gold and her frock of blue, danced before me round corners and pattered down passages, I had the view of a castle of romance inhabited by a rosy sprite, such a place as would somehow, for diversion of the young idea, take all color out of storybooks and fairytales. Wasn't it just a storybook over which I had fallen adoze and adream? No; it was a big, ugly, antique, but convenient house, embodying a few features of a building still older, half-replaced and half-utilized, in which I had the fancy of our being almost as lost as a handful of passengers in a great drifting ship. Well, I was, strangely, at the helm!

Analysis: The governess introduces the imagery of a ship here: imagery which filters in and out of the story. The metaphor gives us a sense of the governess' lack of experience. She describes herself as being "strangely, at the helm". In other words, she realizes that she is in charge: her mixed feelings about being responsible for the children are central to what happens in the narrative.

Discussion point: Why does James use imagery connected with ships during this story?

## Questions

Where is the country house?
What is Flora like: how old, appearance, manners, mood?
What does Mrs Grose say about Flora's brother?
What does the governess do with Flora the next day?
What did the governess then feel about Bly, and what does she feel now?
GCSE style question: how successful is this as the opening of a ghost story?
A Level style question: compare and contrast the opening of this story with another relevant text, exploring the similarities and differences between the texts.
Creative response: write a description of a spooky setting such as a remote house or a derelict building. Try to avoid the normal clichés.
You can find brief answers in the section, **Answers to the Questions**.

# Chapter 2

This came home to me when, two days later, I drove over with Flora to meet, as Mrs. Grose said, the little gentleman; and all the more for an incident that, presenting itself the second evening, had deeply disconcerted me. The first day had been, on the whole, as I have expressed, reassuring; but I was to see it wind up in keen apprehension. The postbag, that evening—it came late—contained a letter for me, which, however, in the hand of my employer, I found to be composed but of a few words enclosing another, addressed to himself, with a seal still unbroken. "This, I recognize, is from the headmaster, and the headmaster's an awful bore. Read him, please; deal with him; but mind you don't report. Not a word. I'm off!" I broke the seal with a great effort—so great a one that I was a long time coming to it; took the unopened missive at last up to my room and only attacked it just before going to bed. I had better have let it wait till morning, for it gave me a second sleepless night. With no counsel to take, the next day, I was full of distress; and it finally got so the better of me that I determined to open myself at least to Mrs. Grose.

"What does it mean? The child's dismissed his school."

She gave me a look that I remarked at the moment; then, visibly, with a quick blankness, seemed to try to take it back. "But aren't they all—?"

"Sent home—yes. But only for the holidays. Miles may never go back at all."

Consciously, under my attention, she reddened. "They won't take him?"

"They absolutely decline."

At this she raised her eyes, which she had turned from me; I saw them fill with good tears. "What has he done?"

I hesitated; then I judged best simply to hand her my letter—which, however, had the effect of making her, without taking it, simply put her hands behind her. She shook her head sadly. "Such things are not for me, miss."

My counselor couldn't read! I winced at my mistake, which I attenuated as I could, and opened my letter again to repeat it to her; then, faltering in the act and folding it up once more, I put it back in my pocket. "Is he really BAD?"

The tears were still in her eyes. "Do the gentlemen say so?"

"They go into no particulars. They simply express their regret that it should be impossible to keep him. That can have only one meaning." Mrs. Grose listened with dumb emotion; she forbore to ask me what this meaning might be; so that, presently, to put the thing with some coherence and with the mere aid of her presence to my own mind, I went on: "That he's an injury to the others."

At this, with one of the quick turns of simple folk, she suddenly flamed up. "Master Miles! HIM an injury?"

There was such a flood of good faith in it that, though I had not yet seen the child, my very fears made me jump to the absurdity of the idea. I found myself, to meet my friend the better, offering it, on the spot, sarcastically. "To his poor little innocent mates!"

"It's too dreadful," cried Mrs. Grose, "to say such cruel things! Why, he's scarce ten years old."

"Yes, yes; it would be incredible."

She was evidently grateful for such a profession. "See him, miss, first. THEN believe it!" I felt forthwith a new impatience to see him; it was the beginning of a curiosity that, for all the next hours, was to deepen almost to pain. Mrs. Grose was aware, I could judge, of what she had produced in me, and she followed it up with assurance. "You might as well believe it of the little lady. Bless her," she added the next moment—"LOOK at her!"

I turned and saw that Flora, whom, ten minutes before, I had established in the schoolroom with a sheet of white paper, a pencil, and a copy of nice "round o's," now presented herself to view at the open door.

### Analysis: Notice here how James presents the governess through his use of dialogue. A repeated trait of the governess is that she jumps to very definite conclusions based on limited or flimsy evidence. This is one of the first examples of this: she says "that could have only meaning, that he's an injury to the others". Here we see how she immediately turns Miles' expulsion from school into a disaster, thinking that he must be a damaging personality. This tendency of hers to "catastrophise" – to turn events into catastrophes – is at the heart why the tragedy happens in this story, and possibly explains why she sees the ghosts. We further see evidence of the governess's unstable nature in the way her desire to meet Miles "deepen(s) almost to pain".

### Discussion point: Why do people like to interpret events in the worst possible light? What are the reasons pupils get expelled from school?

She expressed in her little way an extraordinary detachment from disagreeable duties, looking to me, however, with a great childish light that seemed to offer it as a mere result of the affection she had conceived for my person, which had rendered necessary that she should follow me. I needed nothing more than this to feel the full force of Mrs. Grose's comparison, and, catching my pupil in my arms, covered her with kisses in which there was a sob of atonement.

Nonetheless, the rest of the day I watched for further occasion to approach my colleague, especially as, toward evening, I began to fancy she rather sought to avoid me. I overtook her, I remember, on the staircase; we went down together, and at the bottom I detained her, holding her there with a hand on her arm. "I take what you said to me at noon as a declaration that YOU'VE never known him to be bad."

She threw back her head; she had clearly, by this time, and very honestly, adopted an attitude. "Oh, never known him—I don't pretend THAT!"

I was upset again. "Then you HAVE known him—?"

"Yes indeed, miss, thank God!"

On reflection I accepted this. "You mean that a boy who never is—?"

"Is no boy for ME!"

I held her tighter. "You like them with the spirit to be naughty?" Then, keeping pace with her answer, "So do I!" I eagerly brought out. "But not to the degree to contaminate—"

"To contaminate?"—my big word left her at a loss. I explained it. "To corrupt."

She stared, taking my meaning in; but it produced in her an odd laugh. "Are you afraid he'll corrupt YOU?" She put the question with such a fine bold humor that, with a laugh, a little silly doubtless, to match her own, I gave way for the time to the apprehension of ridicule.

Analysis: The conversations between Mrs Grose and the governess form much of the dynamic of the novel. Here we see a crucial element to them. The governess interrogates Mrs Grose to ask if she truly knows Miles, who replies that she has not known him to be naughty. Then both women agree that it's no good to have a child who is never naughty, but then the governess takes things a step further by suggesting that Miles' naughtiness might "contaminate" and "corrupt". These are two very important verbs: one of the really creepy elements in the book is the way in which James persuades us that there is something "corrupting" and "contaminating" about Miles, despite the fact that we know this is an irrational feeling.

Discussion point: What is "corrupting" behaviour in your view? What do you think the governess means about Miles "contaminating" and "corrupting"?

But the next day, as the hour for my drive approached, I cropped up in another place. "What was the lady who was here before?"

"The last governess? She was also young and pretty—almost as young and almost as pretty, miss, even as you."

"Ah, then, I hope her youth and her beauty helped her!" I recollect throwing off. "He seems to like us young and pretty!"

"Oh, he DID," Mrs. Grose assented: "it was the way he liked everyone!" She had no sooner spoken indeed than she caught herself up. "I mean that's HIS way—the master's."

I was struck. "But of whom did you speak first?"

She looked blank, but she colored. "Why, of HIM."

"Of the master?"

"Of who else?"

There was so obviously no one else that the next moment I had lost my impression of her having accidentally said more than she meant; and I merely asked what I wanted to know. "Did SHE see anything in the boy—?"

"That wasn't right? She never told me."

I had a scruple, but I overcame it. "Was she careful—particular?"

Mrs. Grose appeared to try to be conscientious. "About some things—

yes."

"But not about all?"

Again she considered. "Well, miss—she's gone. I won't tell tales."

"I quite understand your feeling," I hastened to reply; but I thought it, after an instant, not opposed to this concession to pursue: "Did she die here?"

"No—she went off."

## Analysis: James builds suspense by creating a real sense of mystery and sexual intrigue. When the governess says that the absent master "seems to like us young and pretty", we have a sense that she is both attracted and repelled by this notion. Then Mrs Grose disturbs the governess by making a veiled reference to Peter Quint, which she corrects hastily, not wanting to reveal anything about him. Thus we see James beginning to create a real mystery about this anonymous man who lusted after the previous governess. Mrs Grose is very hesitant and vague about events, which makes us wonder what has happened. Notice the way in which James uses pronouns to great effect in the story: "him" is ambiguous. We don't know quite who "him" is here, and this is important in creating suspense.

## Discussion point: Why does Mrs Grose "colour"?

I don't know what there was in this brevity of Mrs. Grose's that struck me as ambiguous. "Went off to die?" Mrs. Grose looked straight out of the window, but I felt that, hypothetically, I had a right to know what young persons engaged for Bly were expected to do. "She was taken ill, you mean, and went home?"

"She was not taken ill, so far as appeared, in this house. She left it, at the end of the year, to go home, as she said, for a short holiday, to which the time she had put in had certainly given her a right. We had then a young woman—a nursemaid who had stayed on and who was a good girl and clever; and SHE took the children altogether for the interval. But our young lady never came back, and at the very moment I was expecting her I heard from the master that she was dead."

I turned this over. "But of what?"

"He never told me! But please, miss," said Mrs. Grose, "I must get to my work."

## Questions

What is enclosed in the uncle's letter to the governess which troubles her?

What is Mrs Grose's response to the news about Miles and the school?

What does Mrs Grose say about Miles's behavior when the governess questions her again?

What does Mrs Grose say about the previous governess who died?

GCSE style question: how does James create a sense of mystery about Miles?

Creative response: write a story about a child who is expelled from school called 'Excluded'. Explore why he/she was expelled; their family set-up; what went wrong.

You can find brief answers in the section, **Answers to the Questions**.

# **Chapter 3**

Her thus turning her back on me was fortunately not, for my just preoccupations, a snub that could check the growth of our mutual esteem. We met, after I had brought home little Miles, more intimately than ever on the ground of my stupefaction, my general emotion: so monstrous was I then ready to pronounce it that such a child as had now been revealed to me should be under an interdict. I was a little late on the scene, and I felt, as he stood wistfully looking out for me before the door of the inn at which the coach had put him down, that I had seen him, on the instant, without and within, in the great glow of freshness, the same positive fragrance of purity, in which I had, from the first moment, seen his little sister. He was incredibly beautiful, and Mrs. Grose had put her finger on it: everything but a sort of passion of tenderness for him was swept away by his presence. What I then and there took him to my heart for was something divine that I have never found to the same degree in any child—his indescribable little air of knowing nothing in the world but love. It would have been impossible to carry a bad name with a greater sweetness of innocence, and by the time I had got back to Bly with him I remained merely bewildered—so far, that is, as I was not outraged—by the sense of the horrible letter locked up in my room, in a drawer. As soon as I could compass a private word with Mrs. Grose I declared to her that it was grotesque.

She promptly understood me. "You mean the cruel charge—?"

"It doesn't live an instant. My dear woman, LOOK at him!"

She smiled at my pretention to have discovered his charm. "I assure you, miss, I do nothing else! What will you say, then?" she immediately added.

"In answer to the letter?" I had made up my mind. "Nothing."

"And to his uncle?"

I was incisive. "Nothing."

"And to the boy himself?"

I was wonderful. "Nothing."

She gave with her apron a great wipe to her mouth. "Then I'll stand by you. We'll see it out."

"We'll see it out!" I ardently echoed, giving her my hand to make it a vow.

She held me there a moment, then whisked up her apron again with her detached hand. "Would you mind, miss, if I used the freedom—"

"To kiss me? No!" I took the good creature in my arms and, after we had embraced like sisters, felt still more fortified and indignant.

This, at all events, was for the time: a time so full that, as I recall the way it went, it reminds me of all the art I now need to make it a little distinct. What I look back at with amazement is the situation I accepted. I had undertaken, with my companion, to see it out, and I was under a charm, apparently, that could smooth away the extent and the far and difficult connections of such an effort. I was lifted aloft on a great wave of infatuation and pity. I found it simple, in my ignorance, my confusion, and perhaps my conceit, to assume that I could deal with a boy whose education for the world was all on the point of beginning. I am unable even to remember at this day what proposal I framed for the end of his holidays and the resumption of his studies. Lessons with me, indeed, that charming summer, we all had a theory that he was to have; but I now feel that, for weeks, the lessons must have been rather my own. I learned something—at first, certainly—that had not been one of the teachings of my small, smothered life; learned to be amused, and even amusing, and not to think for the morrow. It was the first time, in a manner, that I had known space and air and freedom, all the music of summer and all the mystery of nature. And then there was consideration—and consideration was sweet. Oh, it was a trap—not designed, but deep—to my imagination, to my delicacy, perhaps to my vanity; to whatever, in me, was most excitable. The best way to picture it all is to say that I was off my guard. They gave me so little trouble—they were of a gentleness so extraordinary. I used to speculate— but even this with a dim disconnectedness—as to how the rough future (for all futures are rough!) would handle them and might bruise them. They had the bloom of health and happiness; and yet, as if I had been in charge of a pair of little grandees, of princes of the blood, for whom everything, to be right, would have to be enclosed and protected, the only form that, in my fancy, the afteryears could take for them was that of a romantic, a really royal extension of the garden and the park. It may be, of course, above all, that what suddenly broke into this gives the previous time a charm of stillness—that hush in which something gathers or crouches. The change was actually like the spring of a beast.

In the first weeks the days were long; they often, at their finest, gave me what I used to call my own hour, the hour when, for my pupils, teatime and bedtime having come and gone, I had, before my final retirement, a small interval alone. Much as I liked my companions, this hour was the thing in the day I liked most; and I liked it best of all when, as the light faded—or rather, I should say, the day lingered and the last calls of the last birds sounded, in a flushed sky, from the old trees—I could take a turn into the grounds and enjoy, almost with a sense of property that amused and flattered me, the beauty and dignity of the place. It was a pleasure at these moments to feel myself tranquil and justified; doubtless, perhaps, also to reflect that by my discretion, my quiet good sense and general high propriety, I was giving pleasure—if he ever thought of it!—to the person to whose pressure I had responded. What I was doing was what he had earnestly hoped and directly asked of me, and that I COULD, after all, do it proved even a greater joy than I had expected. I daresay I fancied myself, in short, a remarkable young woman and took comfort in the faith that this would more publicly appear. Well, I needed to be remarkable to offer a front to the remarkable things that presently gave their first sign.

It was plump, one afternoon, in the middle of my very hour: the children were tucked away, and I had come out for my stroll. One of the thoughts that, as I don't in the least shrink now from noting, used to be with me in these wanderings was that it would be as charming as a charming story suddenly to meet someone. Someone would appear there at the turn of a path and would stand before me and smile and approve. I didn't ask more than that—I only asked that he should KNOW; and the only way to be sure he knew would be to see it, and the kind light of it, in his handsome face. That was exactly present to me—by which I mean the face was—when, on the first of these occasions, at the end of a long June day, I stopped short on emerging from one of the plantations and coming into view of the house. What arrested me on the spot—and with a shock much greater than any vision had allowed for—was the sense that my imagination had, in a flash, turned real. He did stand there!—but high up, beyond the lawn and at the very top of the tower to which, on that first morning, little Flora had conducted me. This tower was one of a pair—square, incongruous, crenelated structures—that were distinguished, for some reason, though I could see little difference, as the new and the old. They flanked opposite ends of the house and were probably architectural absurdities, redeemed in a measure indeed by not being wholly disengaged nor of a height too pretentious, dating, in their gingerbread antiquity, from a romantic revival that was already a respectable past. I admired them, had fancies about them, for we could all profit in a degree, especially when they loomed through the dusk, by the grandeur of their actual battlements; yet it was not at such an elevation that the figure I had so often invoked seemed most in place.

It produced in me, this figure, in the clear twilight, I remember, two distinct gasps of emotion, which were, sharply, the shock of my first and that of my second surprise. My second was a violent perception of the mistake of my first: the man who met my eyes was not the person I had precipitately supposed. There came to me thus a bewilderment of vision of which, after these years, there is no living view that I can hope to give. An unknown man in a lonely place is a permitted object of fear to a young woman privately bred; and the figure that faced me was—a few more seconds assured me—as little anyone else I knew as it was the image that had been in my mind. I had not seen it in Harley Street—I had not seen it anywhere. The place, moreover, in the strangest way in the world, had, on the instant, and by the very fact of its appearance, become a solitude. To me at least, making my statement here with a deliberation with which I have never made it, the whole feeling of the moment returns. It was as if, while I took in—what I did take in—all the rest of the scene had been stricken with death. I can hear again, as I write, the intense hush in which the sounds of evening dropped. The rooks stopped cawing in the golden sky, and the friendly hour lost, for the minute, all its voice. But there was no other change in nature, unless indeed it were a change that I saw with a stranger sharpness. The gold was still in the sky, the clearness in the air, and the man who looked at me over the battlements was as definite as a picture in a frame. That's how I thought, with extraordinary quickness, of each person that he might have been and that he was not. We were confronted across our distance quite long enough for me to ask myself with intensity who then he was and to feel, as an effect of my inability to say, a wonder that in a few instants more became intense.

> Analysis: This is the first sighting of a ghost. It is important to look closely at it because it shows James breaking many conventions of the ghost story: the sighting does not happen at night but in daylight, amidst the "golden sky". However, there is an important moment of silence: "an intense hush". James uses silence to great effect in the story: the ghosts often appear at moments of apparent peace; not during great storms as is the convention. Moreover, at this point, the governess is not certain whether it is a ghost at all: her eyes connect with the ghost, making him vividly human, not the eyeless ghosts of the traditional spooky stories.

> Discussion point: How effective is this description of the first sighting of Peter Quint? Do you find it chilling? If so, what is scary about it?

The great question, or one of these, is, afterward, I know, with regard to certain matters, the question of how long they have lasted. Well, this matter of mine, think what you will of it, lasted while I caught at a dozen possibilities, none of which made a difference for the better, that I could see, in there having been in the house—and for how long, above all?—a person of whom I was in ignorance. It lasted while I just bridled a little with the sense that my office demanded that there should be no such ignorance and no such person. It lasted while this visitant, at all events— and there was a touch of the strange freedom, as I remember, in the sign of familiarity of his wearing no hat—seemed to fix me, from his position, with just the question, just the scrutiny through the fading light, that his own presence provoked. We were too far apart to call to each other, but there was a moment at which, at shorter range, some challenge between us, breaking the hush, would have been the right result of our straight mutual stare. He was in one of the angles, the one away from the house, very erect, as it struck me, and with both hands on the ledge. So I saw him as I see the letters I form on this page; then, exactly, after a minute, as if to add to the spectacle, he slowly changed his place—passed, looking at me hard all the while, to the opposite corner of the platform. Yes, I had the sharpest sense that during this transit he never took his eyes from me, and I can see at this moment the way his hand, as he went, passed from one of the crenelations to the next. He stopped at the other corner, but less long, and even as he turned away still markedly fixed me. He turned away; that was all I knew.

## Questions

What does the governess feel about Miles when she sees him and why? What does she decide to do about Miles's expulsion?

What is the behavior of the children like?

What does the governess see when she goes for a walk one evening?

What do you think Miles did wrong at school?

GCSE style question: how does James make the appearance of Peter Quint so disturbing and different from most other ghost scenes?

A Level style question: compare and contrast this first sighting of a ghost with another first sighting of a ghost/horrifying thing in another relevant text.

Creative response: write Miles's diary about why he was expelled from school.

Creative response: write a description of someone who sees a ghost for the first time.

You can find brief answers in the section, **Answers to the Questions**.

# Chapter 4

It was not that I didn't wait, on this occasion, for more, for I was rooted as deeply as I was shaken. Was there a "secret" at Bly—a mystery of Udolpho or an insane, an unmentionable relative kept in unsuspected confinement? I can't say how long I turned it over, or how long, in a confusion of curiosity and dread, I remained where I had had my collision; I only recall that when I re-entered the house darkness had quite closed in. Agitation, in the interval, certainly had held me and driven me, for I must, in circling about the place, have walked three miles; but I was to be, later on, so much more overwhelmed that this mere dawn of alarm was a comparatively human chill. The most singular part of it, in fact—singular as the rest had been—was the part I became, in the hall, aware of in meeting Mrs. Grose. This picture comes back to me in the general train—the impression, as I received it on my return, of the wide white panelled space, bright in the lamplight and with its portraits and red carpet, and of the good surprised look of my friend, which immediately told me she had missed me. It came to me straightway, under her contact, that, with plain heartiness, mere relieved anxiety at my appearance, she knew nothing whatever that could bear upon the incident I had there ready for her. I had not suspected in advance that her comfortable face would pull me up, and I somehow measured the importance of what I had seen by my thus finding myself hesitate to mention it. Scarce anything in the whole history seems to me so odd as this fact that my real beginning of fear was one, as I may say, with the instinct of sparing my companion. On the spot, accordingly, in the pleasant hall and with her eyes on me, I, for a reason that I couldn't then have phrased, achieved an inward resolution—offered a vague pretext for my lateness and, with the plea of the beauty of the night and of the heavy dew and wet feet, went as soon as possible to my room.

Here it was another affair; here, for many days after, it was a queer affair enough. There were hours, from day to day—or at least there were moments, snatched even from clear duties—when I had to shut myself up to think. It was not so much yet that I was more nervous than I could bear to be as that I was remarkably afraid of becoming so; for the truth I had now to turn over was, simply and clearly, the truth that I could arrive at no account whatever of the visitor with whom I had been so inexplicably and yet, as it seemed to me, so intimately concerned. It took little time to see that I could sound without forms of inquiry and without exciting remark any domestic complications. The shock I had suffered must have sharpened all my senses; I felt sure, at the end of three days and as the result of mere closer attention, that I had not been practiced upon by the servants nor made the object of any "game." Of whatever it was that I knew, nothing was known around me. There was but one sane inference: someone had taken a liberty rather gross. That was what, repeatedly, I dipped into my room and locked the door to say to myself. We had been, collectively, subject to an intrusion; some unscrupulous traveler, curious in old houses, had made his way in unobserved, enjoyed the prospect from the best point of view, and then stolen out as he came. If he had given me such a bold hard stare, that was but a part of his indiscretion. The good thing, after all, was that we should surely see no more of him.

This was not so good a thing, I admit, as not to leave me to judge that what, essentially, made nothing else much signify was simply my charming work. My charming work was just my life with Miles and Flora, and through nothing could I so like it as through feeling that I could throw myself into it in trouble. The attraction of my small charges was a constant joy, leading me to wonder afresh at the vanity of my original fears, the distaste I had begun by entertaining for the probable gray prose of my office. There was to be no gray prose, it appeared, and no long grind; so how could work not be charming that presented itself as daily beauty? It was all the romance of the nursery and the poetry of the schoolroom. I don't mean by this, of course, that we studied only fiction and verse; I mean I can express no otherwise the sort of interest my companions inspired. How can I describe that except by saying that instead of growing used to them—and it's a marvel for a governess: I call the sisterhood to witness!—I made constant fresh discoveries. There was one direction, assuredly, in which these discoveries stopped: deep obscurity continued to cover the region of the boy's conduct at school. It had been promptly given me, I have noted, to face that mystery without a pang. Perhaps even it would be nearer the truth to say that—without a word—he himself had cleared it up. He had made the whole charge absurd. My conclusion bloomed there with the real rose flush of his innocence: he was only too fine and fair for the little horrid, unclean school world, and he had paid a price for it. I reflected acutely that the sense of such differences, such superiorities of quality, always, on the part of the majority—which could include even stupid, sordid headmasters—turn infallibly to the vindictive.

Both the children had a gentleness (it was their only fault, and it never made Miles a muff) that kept them—how shall I express it?—almost impersonal and certainly quite unpunishable. They were like the cherubs of the anecdote, who had—morally, at any rate—nothing to whack! I remember feeling with Miles in especial as if he had had, as it were, no history. We expect of a small child a scant one, but there was in this beautiful little boy something extraordinarily sensitive, yet extraordinarily happy, that, more than in any creature of his age I have seen, struck me as beginning anew each day. He had never for a second suffered. I took this as a direct disproof of his having really been chastised. If he had been wicked he would have "caught" it, and I should have caught it by the rebound—I should have found the trace. I found nothing at all, and he was therefore an angel. He never spoke of his school, never mentioned a comrade or a master; and I, for my part, was quite too much disgusted to allude to them. Of course I was under the spell, and the wonderful part is that, even at the time, I perfectly knew I was. But I gave myself up to it; it was an antidote to any pain, and I had more pains than one. I was in receipt in these days of disturbing letters from home, where things were not going well. But with my children, what things in the world mattered? That was the question I used to put to my scrappy retirements. I was dazzled by their loveliness.

Analysis: James manages to build more suspense by making the children very well behaved. There is something terrifyingly unreal about them being "unpunishable". The governess' description of being "dazzled by their loveliness" is interesting because it almost gives us a sense that she can't see them properly because of their charm: she is "dazzled", blinded almost.

Discussion point: Why does James describe the children as being "impersonal"?

There was a Sunday—to get on—when it rained with such force and for so many hours that there could be no procession to church; in consequence of which, as the day declined, I had arranged with Mrs. Grose that, should the evening show improvement, we would attend together the late service. The rain happily stopped, and I prepared for our walk, which, through the park and by the good road to the village, would be a matter of twenty minutes. Coming downstairs to meet my colleague in the hall, I remembered a pair of gloves that had required three stitches and that had received them—with a publicity perhaps not edifying—while I sat with the children at their tea, served on Sundays, by exception, in that cold, clean temple of mahogany and brass, the "grown-up" dining room. The gloves had been dropped there, and I turned in to recover them. The day was gray enough, but the afternoon light still lingered, and it enabled me, on crossing the threshold, not only to recognize, on a chair near the wide window, then closed, the articles I wanted, but to become aware of a person on the other side of the window and looking straight in. One step into the room had sufficed; my vision was instantaneous; it was all there. The person looking straight in was the person who had already appeared to me. He appeared thus again with I won't say greater distinctness, for that was impossible, but with a nearness that represented a forward stride in our intercourse and made me, as I met him, catch my breath and turn cold. He was the same—he was the same, and seen, this time, as he had been seen before, from the waist up, the window, though the dining room was on the ground floor, not going down to the terrace on which he stood. His face was close to the glass, yet the effect of this better view was, strangely, only to show me how intense the former had been. He remained but a few seconds—long enough to convince me he also saw and recognized; but it was as if I had been looking at him for years and had known him always. Something, however, happened this time that had not happened before; his stare into my face, through the glass and across the room, was as deep and hard as then, but it quitted me for a moment during which I could still watch it, see it fix successively several other things. On the spot there came to me the added shock of a certitude that it was not for me he had come there. He had come for someone else.

The flash of this knowledge—for it was knowledge in the midst of dread— produced in me the most extraordinary effect, started as I stood there, a sudden vibration of duty and courage. I say courage because I was beyond all doubt already far gone. I bounded straight out of the door again, reached that of the house, got, in an instant, upon the drive, and, passing along the terrace as fast as I could rush, turned a corner and came full in sight. But it was in sight of nothing now—my visitor had vanished.

> ## Analysis: The second sighting of Peter Quint is creepier than the first for a number of reasons. Firstly, the governess responds much more intensely towards him. She says: "it was as if I had been looking at him for years and had known him always", which creates real drama because there is something hugely familiar about the ghost, begging the questions: what is familiar about him? Why does she feel she has known him always? There is something very intimate about her reaction to him: she responds to him like a person who has fallen in love with a stranger might respond. This response gives an extra twist and frisson of feeling for the sentence that follows: "He had come for someone else". In other words, there is a sense that she is disappointed by his not coming for her. Her reaction is extreme: she has a "flash of dread" which turns into a "sudden vibration of duty and courage". James' language is brilliant at conveying the bodily sensations she has, making her belief in the ghosts all the more convincing.

**Discussion point:** Why do you think the governess has a "sudden vibration of duty and courage"?

I stopped, I almost dropped, with the real relief of this; but I took in the whole scene—I gave him time to reappear. I call it time, but how long was it? I can't speak to the purpose today of the duration of these things. That kind of measure must have left me: they couldn't have lasted as they actually appeared to me to last. The terrace and the whole place, the lawn and the garden beyond it, all I could see of the park, were empty with a great emptiness. There were shrubberies and big trees, but I remember the clear assurance I felt that none of them concealed him. He was there or was not there: not there if I didn't see him. I got hold of this; then, instinctively, instead of returning as I had come, went to the window. It was confusedly present to me that I ought to place myself where he had stood. I did so; I applied my face to the pane and looked, as he had looked, into the room. As if, at this moment, to show me exactly what his range had been, Mrs. Grose, as I had done for himself just before, came in from the hall. With this I had the full image of a repetition of what had already occurred. She saw me as I had seen my own visitant; she pulled up short as I had done; I gave her something of the shock that I had received. She turned white, and this made me ask myself if I had blanched as much. She stared, in short, and retreated on just MY lines, and I knew she had then passed out and come round to me and that I should presently meet her. I remained where I was, and while I waited I thought of more things than one. But there's only one I take space to mention. I wondered why SHE should be scared.

## Questions

Why does the governess think Miles was expelled from the school?
What troubles the governess about the children?
What does the governess see at the window one Sunday?
What does the governess do?
What startles Mrs Grose?
GCSE style question: how does James make the second sighting of the ghost so exciting and confusing?
Creative response: write a description of a child who is odd or strange to an adult in some way.
You can find brief answers in the section, **Answers to the Questions**.

# Chapter 5

Oh, she let me know as soon as, round the corner of the house, she loomed again into view. "What in the name of goodness is the matter—?" She was now flushed and out of breath.

I said nothing till she came quite near. "With me?" I must have made a wonderful face. "Do I show it?"

"You're as white as a sheet. You look awful."

I considered; I could meet on this, without scruple, any innocence. My need to respect the bloom of Mrs. Grose's had dropped, without a rustle, from my shoulders, and if I wavered for the instant it was not with what I kept back. I put out my hand to her and she took it; I held her hard a little, liking to feel her close to me. There was a kind of support in the shy heave of her surprise. "You came for me for church, of course, but I can't go."

"Has anything happened?"

"Yes. You must know now. Did I look very queer?"

"Through this window? Dreadful!"

"Well," I said, "I've been frightened." Mrs. Grose's eyes expressed plainly that SHE had no wish to be, yet also that she knew too well her place not to be ready to share with me any marked inconvenience. Oh, it was quite settled that she MUST share! "Just what you saw from the dining room a minute ago was the effect of that. What I saw—just before—was much worse."

Her hand tightened. "What was it?"

"An extraordinary man. Looking in."

"What extraordinary man?"

"I haven't the least idea."

Mrs. Grose gazed round us in vain. "Then where is he gone?"

"I know still less."

"Have you seen him before?"

"Yes—once. On the old tower."

She could only look at me harder. "Do you mean he's a stranger?"

Analysis: This tense dialogue between Mrs Grose and the governess is effective because of its brevity. The governess' choice of adjective to describe Quint is interesting: she describes him as "extraordinary", almost as if she is deeply impressed by him.

Discussion point: What do you think Mrs Grose is thinking at this point?

"Oh, very much!"

"Yet you didn't tell me?"

"No—for reasons. But now that you've guessed—"

Mrs. Grose's round eyes encountered this charge. "Ah, I haven't guessed!" she said very simply. "How can I if YOU don't imagine?"

"I don't in the very least."

"You've seen him nowhere but on the tower?"

"And on this spot just now."

Mrs. Grose looked round again. "What was he doing on the tower?"

"Only standing there and looking down at me."

She thought a minute. "Was he a gentleman?"

I found I had no need to think. "No." She gazed in deeper wonder. "No."

"Then nobody about the place? Nobody from the village?"

"Nobody—nobody. I didn't tell you, but I made sure."

She breathed a vague relief: this was, oddly, so much to the good. It only went indeed a little way. "But if he isn't a gentleman—"

"What IS he? He's a horror."

"A horror?"

"He's—God help me if I know WHAT he is!"

Mrs. Grose looked round once more; she fixed her eyes on the duskier distance, then, pulling herself together, turned to me with abrupt inconsequence. "It's time we should be at church."

"Oh, I'm not fit for church!"

"Won't it do you good?"

"It won't do THEM—! I nodded at the house.

"The children?"

"I can't leave them now."

"You're afraid—?"

I spoke boldly. "I'm afraid of HIM."

Mrs. Grose's large face showed me, at this, for the first time, the faraway faint glimmer of a consciousness more acute: I somehow made out in it the delayed dawn of an idea I myself had not given her and that was as yet quite obscure to me. It comes back to me that I thought instantly of this as something I could get from her; and I felt it to be connected with the desire she presently showed to know more. "When was it—on the tower?"

"About the middle of the month. At this same hour."

"Almost at dark," said Mrs. Grose.

"Oh, no, not nearly. I saw him as I see you."

"Then how did he get in?"

"And how did he get out?" I laughed. "I had no opportunity to ask him! This evening, you see," I pursued, "he has not been able to get in."

"He only peeps?"

"I hope it will be confined to that!" She had now let go my hand; she turned away a little. I waited an instant; then I brought out: "Go to church. Goodbye. I must watch."

Slowly she faced me again. "Do you fear for them?"

We met in another long look. "Don't YOU?" Instead of answering she came nearer to the window and, for a minute, applied her face to the glass. "You see how he could see," I meanwhile went on.

She didn't move. "How long was he here?"

"Till I came out. I came to meet him."

Mrs. Grose at last turned round, and there was still more in her face. "I couldn't have come out."

"Neither could I!" I laughed again. "But I did come. I have my duty."

"So have I mine," she replied; after which she added: "What is he like?"

"I've been dying to tell you. But he's like nobody."

"Nobody?" she echoed.

"He has no hat." Then seeing in her face that she already, in this, with a deeper dismay, found a touch of picture, I quickly added stroke to stroke. "He has red hair, very red, close-curling, and a pale face, long in shape, with straight, good features and little, rather queer whiskers that are as red as his hair. His eyebrows are, somehow, darker; they look particularly arched and as if they might move a good deal. His eyes are sharp, strange—awfully; but I only know clearly that they're rather small and very fixed. His mouth's wide, and his lips are thin, and except for his little whiskers he's quite clean-shaven. He gives me a sort of sense of looking like an actor."

"An actor!" It was impossible to resemble one less, at least, than Mrs. Grose at that moment.

"I've never seen one, but so I suppose them. He's tall, active, erect," I continued, "but never—no, never!—a gentleman."

My companion's face had blanched as I went on; her round eyes started and her mild mouth gaped. "A gentleman?" she gasped, confounded, stupefied: "a gentleman HE?"

"You know him then?"

She visibly tried to hold herself. "But he IS handsome?"

I saw the way to help her. "Remarkably!"

"And dressed—?"

"In somebody's clothes." "They're smart, but they're not his own."

She broke into a breathless affirmative groan: "They're the master's!"

I caught it up. "You DO know him?"

She faltered but a second. "Quint!" she cried.

"Quint?"

"Peter Quint—his own man, his valet, when he was here!"

"When the master was?"

Gaping still, but meeting me, she pieced it all together. "He never wore his hat, but he did wear—well, there were waistcoats missed. They were both here—last year. Then the master went, and Quint was alone."

I followed, but halting a little. "Alone?"

"Alone with US." Then, as from a deeper depth, "In charge," she added.

"And what became of him?"

She hung fire so long that I was still more mystified. "He went, too," she brought out at last.

"Went where?"

Her expression, at this, became extraordinary. "God knows where! He died."

"Died?" I almost shrieked.

She seemed fairly to square herself, plant herself more firmly to utter the wonder of it. "Yes. Mr. Quint is dead."

Analysis: The revelation that the vision the governess saw is really the ghost of Peter Quint is very important to analyse. Firstly, it is important that the governess admits to finding her vision "remarkably" handsome is significant in that we realise now that she was attracted by the ghost. Twentieth century critics have argued that this indicates that Quint could be a product of the governess' sexually repressed imagination, a hallucination which has happened because she is a frustrated, neurotic woman who is not sexually fulfilled. There is some evidence for this argument here: she "shrieks" when she hears that Quint was dead, indicating her emotional state of mind, which contrasts with Mrs Grose's more measured mystification. However, there is some evidence here to suggest that the governess is not mad: she saw Quint before she knew about, seeing that he had red hair and wearing clothes belonging to the master which she couldn't have possibly known about beforehand. In other words, she did not see a vague vision which she has feverishly interpreted as being a ghost: she has seen a very distinct vision which quite definitely matches the description of Quint.

Discussion point: How does James create suspense in the above passage? Do you think James is suggesting that she saw a real ghost or does he drop enough hints that the ghost is a product of her fevered, unbalanced imagination?

## Questions

What does the governess confess to Mrs Grose?

Why does the governess feel she can't go to church?

What does the governess say the intruder looked like after being questioned by Mrs Grose?

Who does Mrs Grose say this person is like?

GCSE style question: How does James make the conversation between Mrs Grose and the governess so dramatic?

Creative response: write a description of someone who sees an intruder on their property; what do they think or feel?

You can find brief answers in the section, **Answers to the Questions**.

# Chapter 6

It took of course more than that particular passage to place us together in presence of what we had now to live with as we could—my dreadful liability to impressions of the order so vividly exemplified, and my companion's knowledge, henceforth—a knowledge half consternation and half compassion—of that liability. There had been, this evening, after the revelation left me, for an hour, so prostrate—there had been, for either of us, no attendance on any service but a little service of tears and vows, of prayers and promises, a climax to the series of mutual challenges and pledges that had straightway ensued on our retreating together to the schoolroom and shutting ourselves up there to have everything out. The result of our having everything out was simply to reduce our situation to the last rigor of its elements. She herself had seen nothing, not the shadow of a shadow, and nobody in the house but the governess was in the governess's plight; yet she accepted without directly impugning my sanity the truth as I gave it to her, and ended by showing me, on this ground, an awestricken tenderness, an expression of the sense of my more than questionable privilege, of which the very breath has remained with me as that of the sweetest of human charities.

What was settled between us, accordingly, that night, was that we thought we might bear things together; and I was not even sure that, in spite of her exemption, it was she who had the best of the burden. I knew at this hour, I think, as well as I knew later, what I was capable of meeting to shelter my pupils; but it took me some time to be wholly sure of what my honest ally was prepared for to keep terms with so compromising a contract. I was queer company enough—quite as queer as the company I received; but as I trace over what we went through I see how much common ground we must have found in the one idea that, by good fortune, COULD steady us. It was the idea, the second movement, that led me straight out, as I may say, of the inner chamber of my dread. I could take the air in the court, at least, and there Mrs. Grose could join me. Perfectly can I recall now the particular way strength came to me before we separated for the night. We had gone over and over every feature of what I had seen.

"He was looking for someone else, you say—someone who was not you?"

"He was looking for little Miles." A portentous clearness now possessed me. "THAT'S whom he was looking for."

"But how do you know?"

"I know, I know, I know!" My exaltation grew. "And YOU know, my dear!"

She didn't deny this, but I required, I felt, not even so much telling as that. She resumed in a moment, at any rate: "What if HE should see him?"

"Little Miles? That's what he wants!"

She looked immensely scared again. "The child?"

## Analysis: Here we see the governess beginning to jump to conclusions. We have no evidence that the ghost is looking for Miles other than her intuition that he is. James' presentation of this is fascinating: he describes her as being "possessed" by a "portentous clearness". He is describes her in the same way a religious person might describe someone being "possessed" by the devil. Except she is possessed by a "clearness". Her narrative is persuasive, but perhaps this is where the governess goes wrong. Perhaps there were really ghosts, but they hadn't come for the children at all. Her first sighting of Quint indicates that he had initially come for her, something that her repressed nature couldn't endure. Furthermore, we see the governess become even more unbalanced as she begins to believe her own perceptions with more conviction after talking to Mrs Grose. Her "exaltation" grows. This abstract noun is fascinating because it has religious connotations: she is exalted like a holy man by her knowledge of what the ghost wants. In other words, she casts the ghost as a devil and herself as a saviour. She perceives herself as battling against evil, and feels greatly energised by this concept. Finally, she has an important role to play. She is no longer an ordinary governess, teaching a couple of rich children, but she is someone who is discovering real evil.

## Discussion point: What evidence is there that Mrs Grose is rather sceptical?

"Heaven forbid! The man. He wants to appear to THEM." That he might was an awful conception, and yet, somehow, I could keep it at bay; which, moreover, as we lingered there, was what I succeeded in practically proving. I had an absolute certainty that I should see again what I had already seen, but something within me said that by offering myself bravely as the sole subject of such experience, by accepting, by inviting, by surmounting it all, I should serve as an expiatory victim and guard the tranquility of my companions. The children, in especial, I should thus fence about and absolutely save. I recall one of the last things I said that night to Mrs. Grose.

"It does strike me that my pupils have never mentioned—"

She looked at me hard as I musingly pulled up. "His having been here and the time they were with him?"

"The time they were with him, and his name, his presence, his history, in any way."

"Oh, the little lady doesn't remember. She never heard or knew."

"The circumstances of his death?" I thought with some intensity. "Perhaps not. But Miles would remember—Miles would know."

"Ah, don't try him!" broke from Mrs. Grose.

I returned her the look she had given me. "Don't be afraid." I continued to think. "It IS rather odd."

"That he has never spoken of him?"

"Never by the least allusion. And you tell me they were 'great friends'?"

"Oh, it wasn't HIM!" Mrs. Grose with emphasis declared. "It was Quint's own fancy. To play with him, I mean—to spoil him." She paused a moment; then she added: "Quint was much too free."

This gave me, straight from my vision of his face—SUCH a face!—a sudden sickness of disgust. "Too free with MY boy?"

> Analysis: Here we see as the governess learns more about the past, she builds upon the scenario that she has already begun to shape for herself: that she must save the children from the evil ghost. Mrs Grose's comments are guarded, but we see the clever governess snatch at the trifling evidence to build her own case. Her question, "Too free with *my* boy" is very important because it reveals two things. Firstly the notion that Quint encouraged the boy to be "free" or "licentious", in other words Quint allowed the boy's evil side free reign. Secondly, we see the governess's insecure possessiveness: Miles has become "*my* boy".

> Discussion point: Look at the way James describes the governess's feelings. What are those feelings and why does James present the governess in this way?

"Too free with everyone!"

I forbore, for the moment, to analyze this description further than by the reflection that a part of it applied to several of the members of the household, of the half-dozen maids and men who were still of our small colony. But there was everything, for our apprehension, in the lucky fact that no discomfortable legend, no perturbation of scullions, had ever, within anyone's memory attached to the kind old place. It had neither bad name nor ill fame, and Mrs. Grose, most apparently, only desired to cling to me and to quake in silence. I even put her, the very last thing of all, to the test. It was when, at midnight, she had her hand on the schoolroom door to take leave. "I have it from you then—for it's of great importance—that he was definitely and admittedly bad?"

"Oh, not admittedly. I knew it—but the master didn't."

"And you never told him?"

"Well, he didn't like tale-bearing—he hated complaints. He was terribly short with anything of that kind, and if people were all right to HIM—"

"He wouldn't be bothered with more?" This squared well enough with my impressions of him: he was not a trouble-loving gentleman, nor so very particular perhaps about some of the company HE kept. All the same, I pressed my interlocutress. "I promise you Iwould have told!"

She felt my discrimination. "I daresay I was wrong. But, really, I was afraid."

"Afraid of what?"

"Of things that man could do. Quint was so clever—he was so deep."

I took this in still more than, probably, I showed. "You weren't afraid of anything else? Not of his effect—?"

"His effect?" she repeated with a face of anguish and waiting while I faltered.

"On innocent little precious lives. They were in your charge."

"No, they were not in mine!" she roundly and distressfully returned. "The master believed in him and placed him here because he was supposed not to be well and the country air so good for him. So he had everything to say. Yes"—she let me have it—"even about THEM."

"Them—that creature?" I had to smother a kind of howl. "And you could bear it!"

"No. I couldn't—and I can't now!" And the poor woman burst into tears.

A rigid control, from the next day, was, as I have said, to follow them; yet how often and how passionately, for a week, we came back together to the subject! Much as we had discussed it that Sunday night, I was, in the immediate later hours in especial—for it may be imagined whether I slept—still haunted with the shadow of something she had not told me. I myself had kept back nothing, but there was a word Mrs. Grose had kept back. I was sure, moreover, by morning, that this was not from a failure of frankness, but because on every side there were fears. It seems to me indeed, in retrospect, that by the time the morrow's sun was high I had restlessly read into the fact before us almost all the meaning they were to receive from subsequent and more cruel occurrences. What they gave me above all was just the sinister figure of the living man—the dead one would keep awhile!—and of the months he had continuously passed at Bly, which, added up, made a formidable stretch. The limit of this evil time had arrived only when, on the dawn of a winter's morning, Peter Quint was found, by a laborer going to early work, stone dead on the road from the village: a catastrophe explained—superficially at least—by a visible wound to his head; such a wound as might have been produced—and as, on the final evidence, HAD been—by a fatal slip, in the dark and after leaving the public house, on the steepish icy slope, a wrong path altogether, at the bottom of which he lay. The icy slope, the turn mistaken at night and in liquor, accounted for much—practically, in the end and after the inquest and boundless chatter, for everything; but there had been matters in his life—strange passages and perils, secret disorders, vices more than suspected—that would have accounted for a good deal more.

I scarce know how to put my story into words that shall be a credible picture of my state of mind; but I was in these days literally able to find a joy in the extraordinary flight of heroism the occasion demanded of me. I now saw that I had been asked for a service admirable and difficult; and there would be a greatness in letting it be seen—oh, in the right quarter!—that I could succeed where many another girl might have failed. It was an immense help to me—I confess I rather applaud myself as I look back!—that I saw my service so strongly and so simply. I was there to protect and defend the little creatures in the world the most bereaved and the most lovable, the appeal of whose helplessness had suddenly become only too explicit, a deep, constant ache of one's own committed heart. We were cut off, really, together; we were united in our danger. They had nothing but me, and I—well, I had THEM. It was in short a magnificent chance. This chance presented itself to me in an image richly material. I was a screen—I was to stand before them. The more I saw, the less they would. I began to watch them in a stifled suspense, a disguised excitement that might well, had it continued too long, have turned to something like madness. What saved me, as I now see, was that it turned to something else altogether. It didn't last as suspense—it was superseded by horrible proofs. Proofs, I say, yes—from the moment I really took hold.

This moment dated from an afternoon hour that I happened to spend in the grounds with the younger of my pupils alone. We had left Miles indoors, on the red cushion of a deep window seat; he had wished to finish a book, and I had been glad to encourage a purpose so laudable in a young man whose only defect was an occasional excess of the restless. His sister, on the contrary, had been alert to come out, and I strolled with her half an hour, seeking the shade, for the sun was still high and the day exceptionally warm. I was aware afresh, with her, as we went, of how, like her brother, she contrived—it was the charming thing in both children—to let me alone without appearing to drop me and to accompany me without appearing to surround. They were never importunate and yet never listless. My attention to them all really went to seeing them amuse themselves immensely without me: this was a spectacle they seemed actively to prepare and that engaged me as an active admirer. I walked in a world of their invention—they had no occasion whatever to draw upon mine; so that my time was taken only with being, for them, some remarkable person or thing that the game of the moment required and that was merely, thanks to my superior, my exalted stamp, a happy and highly distinguished sinecure. I forget what I was on the present occasion; I only remember that I was something very important and very quiet and that Flora was playing very hard. We were on the edge of the lake, and, as we had lately begun geography, the lake was the Sea of Azof.

Suddenly, in these circumstances, I became aware that, on the other side of the Sea of Azof, we had an interested spectator. The way this knowledge gathered in me was the strangest thing in the world—the strangest, that is, except the very much stranger in which it quickly merged itself. I had sat down with a piece of work—for I was something or other that could sit—on the old stone bench which overlooked the pond; and in this position I began to take in with certitude, and yet without direct vision, the presence, at a distance, of a third person. The old trees, the thick shrubbery, made a great and pleasant shade, but it was all suffused with the brightness of the hot, still hour. There was no ambiguity in anything; none whatever, at least, in the conviction I from one moment to another found myself forming as to what I should see straight before me and across the lake as a consequence of raising my eyes. They were attached at this juncture to the stitching in which I was engaged, and I can feel once more the spasm of my effort not to move them till I should so have steadied myself as to be able to make up my mind what to do. There was an alien object in view—a figure whose right of presence I instantly, passionately questioned. I recollect counting over perfectly the possibilities, reminding myself that nothing was more natural, for instance, then the appearance of one of the men about the place, or even of a messenger, a postman, or a tradesman's boy, from the village. That reminder had as little effect on my practical certitude as I was conscious—still even without looking—of its having upon the character and attitude of our visitor. Nothing was more natural than that these things should be the other things that they absolutely were not.

Of the positive identity of the apparition I would assure myself as soon as the small clock of my courage should have ticked out the right second; meanwhile, with an effort that was already sharp enough, I transferred my eyes straight to little Flora, who, at the moment, was about ten yards away. My heart had stood still for an instant with the wonder and terror of the question whether she too would see; and I held my breath while I waited for what a cry from her, what some sudden innocent sign either of interest or of alarm, would tell me. I waited, but nothing came; then, in the first place—and there is something more dire in this, I feel, than in anything I have to relate—I was determined by a sense that, within a minute, all sounds from her had previously dropped; and, in the second, by the circumstance that, also within the minute, she had, in her play, turned her back to the water.

Analysis: Now certain that the ghost is after Miles, wishing to corrupt him, the governess becomes even more possessive of the children, not letting them out of her sight. Then one day, while she is at the lake with Flora, she sees a woman dressed in black and senses that it is Miss Jessel, the governess who preceded her. Here, James creates suspense by having the governess observe Flora with the ghost, wondering whether there will be a "cry from her". We and the governess await a shriek from Flora but nothing comes. Indeed Flora's utter lack of concern seems all the more haunting: is it the case that Flora is so familiar with the ghost that she doesn't need to cry out, or is it that she just can't see her?

## Discussion point: Why does James now introduce a new ghost, Miss Jessel, do you think? Why is she dressed in black?

This was her attitude when I at last looked at her—looked with the confirmed conviction that we were still, together, under direct personal notice. She had picked up a small flat piece of wood, which happened to have in it a little hole that had evidently suggested to her the idea of sticking in another fragment that might figure as a mast and make the thing a boat. This second morsel, as I watched her, she was very markedly and intently attempting to tighten in its place. My apprehension of what she was doing sustained me so that after some seconds I felt I was ready for more. Then I again shifted my eyes—I faced what I had to face.

## Questions

What does the governess suddenly realise about Quint as she discusses things with Mrs Grose?

What does the governess wonder about Miles?

What does Mrs Grose say Quint's behavior was like with Miles?

What does the governess come to see her role has to be at the house?

What does the governess think she sees as she observes Flora playing by the bank of the lake?

Where is Miles at this time?

GCSE style question: How does James make the governess an intriguing and attractive character in this chapter?

Creative response: write a story/description called 'The Rescuer'.

You can find brief answers in the section, **Answers to the Questions**.

# Chapter 7

I got hold of Mrs. Grose as soon after this as I could; and I can give no intelligible account of how I fought out the interval. Yet I still hear myself cry as I fairly threw myself into her arms: "They KNOW—it's too monstrous: they know, they know!"

"And what on earth—?" I felt her incredulity as she held me.

"Why, all that WE know—and heaven knows what else besides!" Then, as she released me, I made it out to her, made it out perhaps only now with full coherency even to myself. "Two hours ago, in the garden"—I could scarce articulate—"Flora SAW!"

Mrs. Grose took it as she might have taken a blow in the stomach. "She has told you?" she panted.

"Not a word—that's the horror. She kept it to herself! The child of eight, THAT child!" Unutterable still, for me, was the stupefaction of it.

Mrs. Grose, of course, could only gape the wider. "Then how do you know?"

"I was there—I saw with my eyes: saw that she was perfectly aware."

"Do you mean aware of HIM?"

"No—of HER." I was conscious as I spoke that I looked prodigious things, for I got the slow reflection of them in my companion's face. "Another person—this time; but a figure of quite as unmistakable horror and evil: a woman in black, pale and dreadful—with such an air also, and such a face!—on the other side of the lake. I was there with the child—quiet for the hour; and in the midst of it she came."

"Came how—from where?"

"From where they come from! She just appeared and stood there—but not so near."

"And without coming nearer?"

"Oh, for the effect and the feeling, she might have been as close as you!"

My friend, with an odd impulse, fell back a step. "Was she someone you've never seen?"

"Yes. But someone the child has. Someone YOU have." Then, to show how I had thought it all out: "My predecessor—the one who died."

"Miss Jessel?"

"Miss Jessel. You don't believe me?" I pressed.

She turned right and left in her distress. "How can you be sure?"

This drew from me, in the state of my nerves, a flash of impatience. "Then ask Flora—SHE'S sure!" But I had no sooner spoken than I caught myself up. "No, for God's sake, DON'T! She'll say she isn't—she'll lie!"

Mrs. Grose was not too bewildered instinctively to protest. "Ah, how CAN you?"

"Because I'm clear. Flora doesn't want me to know."

"It's only then to spare you."

"No, no—there are depths, depths! The more I go over it, the more I see in it, and the more I see in it, the more I fear. I don't know what I DON'T see—what I DON'T fear!"

Mrs. Grose tried to keep up with me. "You mean you're afraid of seeing her again?"

"Oh, no; that's nothing—now!" Then I explained. "It's of NOT seeing her."

But my companion only looked wan. "I don't understand you."

"Why, it's that the child may keep it up—and that the child assuredly WILL—without my knowing it."

At the image of this possibility Mrs. Grose for a moment collapsed, yet presently to pull herself together again, as if from the positive force of the sense of what, should we yield an inch, there would really be to give way to. "Dear, dear—we must keep our heads! And after all, if she doesn't mind it—!" She even tried a grim joke. "Perhaps she likes it!"

"Likes SUCH things—a scrap of an infant!"

"Isn't it just a proof of her blessed innocence?" my friend bravely inquired.

She brought me, for the instant, almost round. "Oh, we must clutch at THAT—we must cling to it! If it isn't a proof of what you say, it's a proof of—God knows what! For the woman's a horror of horrors."

Mrs. Grose, at this, fixed her eyes a minute on the ground; then at last raising them, "Tell me how you know," she said.

"Then you admit it's what she was?" I cried.

"Tell me how you know," my friend simply repeated.

"Know? By seeing her! By the way she looked."

"At you, do you mean—so wickedly?"

"Dear me, no—I could have borne that. She gave me never a glance. She only fixed the child."

Mrs. Grose tried to see it. "Fixed her?"

"Ah, with such awful eyes!"

She stared at mine as if they might really have resembled them. "Do you mean of dislike?"

"God help us, no. Of something much worse."

"Worse than dislike?—this left her indeed at a loss.

"With a determination—indescribable. With a kind of fury of intention."

I made her turn pale. "Intention?"

"To get hold of her." Mrs. Grose—her eyes just lingering on mine—gave a shudder and walked to the window; and while she stood there looking out I completed my statement. "THAT'S what Flora knows."

After a little she turned round. "The person was in black, you say?"

"In mourning—rather poor, almost shabby. But—yes—with extraordinary beauty." I now recognized to what I had at last, stroke by stroke, brought the victim of my confidence, for she quite visibly weighed this. "Oh, handsome—very, very," I insisted; "wonderfully handsome. But infamous."

She slowly came back to me. "Miss Jessel—WAS infamous." She once more took my hand in both her own, holding it as tight as if to fortify me against the increase of alarm I might draw from this disclosure. "They were both infamous," she finally said.

So, for a little, we faced it once more together; and I found absolutely a degree of help in seeing it now so straight. "I appreciate," I said, "the great decency of your not having hitherto spoken; but the time has certainly come to give me the whole thing." She appeared to assent to this, but still only in silence; seeing which I went on: "I must have it now. Of what did she die? Come, there was something between them."

"There was everything."

"In spite of the difference—?"

"Oh, of their rank, their condition"—she brought it woefully out. "SHE was a lady."

I turned it over; I again saw. "Yes—she was a lady."

"And he so dreadfully below," said Mrs. Grose.

I felt that I doubtless needn't press too hard, in such company, on the place of a servant in the scale; but there was nothing to prevent an acceptance of my companion's own measure of my predecessor's abasement. There was a way to deal with that, and I dealt; the more readily for my full vision—on the evidence—of our employer's late clever, good-looking "own" man; impudent, assured, spoiled, depraved. "The fellow was a hound."

Mrs. Grose considered as if it were perhaps a little a case for a sense of shades. "I've never seen one like him. He did what he wished."

"With HER?"

"With them all."

It was as if now in my friend's own eyes Miss Jessel had again appeared. I seemed at any rate, for an instant, to see their evocation of her as distinctly as I had seen her by the pond; and I brought out with decision: "It must have been also what SHE wished!"

Mrs. Grose's face signified that it had been indeed, but she said at the same time: "Poor woman—she paid for it!"

"Then you do know what she died of?" I asked.

"No—I know nothing. I wanted not to know; I was glad enough I didn't; and I thanked heaven she was well out of this!"

"Yet you had, then, your idea—"

"Of her real reason for leaving? Oh, yes—as to that. She couldn't have stayed. Fancy it here—for a governess! And afterward I imagined—and I still imagine. And what I imagine is dreadful."

"Not so dreadful as what I do," I replied; on which I must have shown her—as I was indeed but too conscious—a front of miserable defeat. It brought out again all her compassion for me, and at the renewed touch of her kindness my power to resist broke down. I burst, as I had, the other time, made her burst, into tears; she took me to her motherly breast, and my lamentation overflowed. "I don't do it!" I sobbed in despair; "I don't save or shield them! It's far worse than I dreamed—they're lost!"

Analysis: Here, Mrs Grose reveals more about the past at Bly: we learn that Quint had an affair with Miss Jessel and, as a result, she was forced to leave. As Mrs Grose says: "She couldn't have stayed. Fancy it here – for a governess!" Here the truth is not spoken aloud: this is a deeply repressed society which did not talk openly about sexual liaisons, but instead only alluded to them. This gives them even an even greater grip on the imagination, for as Mrs Grose says: "And afterwards I imagined – and I still imagined. And what I imagine is dreadful." Obviously, she does not explain fully here, but it is clear she is talking about the sexual congress between Quint and Miss Jessel. Not to be outdone, the governess goes one better: "Not so dreadful as what *I* do". The governess imagines the damnation and corruption of the children: "they're lost" because they are in league with the ghosts, imbibing the ghosts' corrupt views, values and ideas. Again, nothing is explicitly stated, but there is a sense that the children are aware of sexual matters that they shouldn't be at a young age. Some critics have felt that the governess imagines them as being sexually abused by the ghosts. The horror here is more intense because we never quite know what the governess imagines is going on.

**Discussion point:** If the ghosts are real and the children can see them, what do you think is going on? If you think the ghosts are not real, then what does this tell us about the governess and Mrs Grose?

## Questions

What does the governess tell Mrs Grose about Flora and Miles?

What does the governess say the ghost looked like?

Who does the governess think this woman is?

How does Mrs Grose defend Flora?

What does Mrs Grose say about Miss Jessel?

What does the governess lament about?

GCSE style question: how does James make the governess's description of the ghost so alarming?

Creative response: imagine you are someone who is told by a close friend/relative that he/she has seen a ghost. Write their account of listening to this sighting of the ghost. Do they believe their friend/relative or not?

Creative response: write Mrs Grose's diary for this chapter.

You can find brief answers in the section, **Answers to the Questions**.

# Chapter 8

What I had said to Mrs. Grose was true enough: there were in the matter I had put before her depths and possibilities that I lacked resolution to sound; so that when we met once more in the wonder of it we were of a common mind about the duty of resistance to extravagant fancies. We were to keep our heads if we should keep nothing else—difficult indeed as that might be in the face of what, in our prodigious experience, was least to be questioned. Late that night, while the house slept, we had another talk in my room, when she went all the way with me as to its being beyond doubt that I had seen exactly what I had seen. To hold her perfectly in the pinch of that, I found I had only to ask her how, if I had "made it up," I came to be able to give, of each of the persons appearing to me, a picture disclosing, to the last detail, their special marks—a portrait on the exhibition of which she had instantly recognized and named them. She wished of course—small blame to her!—to sink the whole subject; and I was quick to assure her that my own interest in it had now violently taken the form of a search for the way to escape from it. I encountered her on the ground of a probability that with recurrence—for recurrence we took for granted—I should get used to my danger, distinctly professing that my personal exposure had suddenly become the least of my discomforts. It was my new suspicion that was intolerable; and yet even to this complication the later hours of the day had brought a little ease.

On leaving her, after my first outbreak, I had of course returned to my pupils, associating the right remedy for my dismay with that sense of their charm which I had already found to be a thing I could positively cultivate and which had never failed me yet. I had simply, in other words, plunged afresh into Flora's special society and there become aware—it was almost a luxury!—that she could put her little conscious hand straight upon the spot that ached. She had looked at me in sweet speculation and then had accused me to my face of having "cried." I had supposed I had brushed away the ugly signs: but I could literally—for the time, at all events— rejoice, under this fathomless charity, that they had not entirely disappeared. To gaze into the depths of blue of the child's eyes and pronounce their loveliness a trick of premature cunning was to be guilty of a cynicism in preference to which I naturally preferred to abjure my judgment and, so far as might be, my agitation. I couldn't abjure for merely wanting to, but I could repeat to Mrs. Grose—as I did there, over and over, in the small hours—that with their voices in the air, their pressure on one's heart, and their fragrant faces against one's cheek, everything fell to the ground but their incapacity and their beauty. It was a pity that, somehow, to settle this once for all, I had equally to re-enumerate the signs of subtlety that, in the afternoon, by the lake had made a miracle of my show of self-possession. It was a pity to be obliged to reinvestigate the certitude of the moment itself and repeat how it had come to me as a revelation that the inconceivable communion I then surprised was a matter, for either party, of habit. It was a pity that I should have had to quaver out again the reasons for my not having, in my delusion, so much as questioned that the little girl saw our visitant even as I actually saw Mrs. Grose herself, and that she wanted, by just so much as she did thus see, to make me suppose she didn't, and at the same time, without showing anything, arrive at a guess as to whether I myself did! It was a pity that I needed once more to describe the portentous little activity by which she sought to divert my attention— the perceptible increase of movement, the greater intensity of play, the singing, the gabbling of nonsense, and the invitation to romp.

Yet if I had not indulged, to prove there was nothing in it, in this review, I should have missed the two or three dim elements of comfort that still remained to me. I should not for instance have been able to asseverate to my friend that I was certain—which was so much to the good—that I at least had not betrayed myself. I should not have been prompted, by stress of need, by desperation of mind—I scarce know what to call it—to invoke such further aid to intelligence as might spring from pushing my colleague fairly to the wall. She had told me, bit by bit, under pressure, a great deal; but a small shifty spot on the wrong side of it all still sometimes brushed my brow like the wing of a bat; and I remember how on this occasion—for the sleeping house and the concentration alike of our danger and our watch seemed to help—I felt the importance of giving the last jerk to the curtain. "I don't believe anything so horrible," I recollect saying; "no, let us put it definitely, my dear, that I don't. But if I did, you know, there's a thing I should require now, just without sparing you the least bit more—oh, not a scrap, come!—to get out of you. What was it you had in mind when, in our distress, before Miles came back, over the letter from his school, you said, under my insistence, that you didn't pretend for him that he had not literally EVER been 'bad'? He has NOT literally 'ever,' in these weeks that I myself have lived with him and so closely watched him; he has been an imperturbable little prodigy of delightful, lovable goodness. Therefore you might perfectly have made the claim for him if you had not, as it happened, seen an exception to take. What was your exception, and to what passage in your personal observation of him did you refer?"

It was a dreadfully austere inquiry, but levity was not our note, and, at any rate, before the gray dawn admonished us to separate I had got my answer. What my friend had had in mind proved to be immensely to the purpose. It was neither more nor less than the circumstance that for a period of several months Quint and the boy had been perpetually together. It was in fact the very appropriate truth that she had ventured to criticize the propriety, to hint at the incongruity, of so close an alliance, and even to go so far on the subject as a frank overture to Miss Jessel. Miss Jessel had, with a most strange manner, requested her to mind her business, and the good woman had, on this, directly approached little Miles. What she had said to him, since I pressed, was that SHE liked to see young gentlemen not forget their station.

I pressed again, of course, at this. "You reminded him that Quint was only a base menial?"

"As you might say! And it was his answer, for one thing, that was bad."

"And for another thing?" I waited. "He repeated your words to Quint?"

"No, not that. It's just what he WOULDN'T!" she could still impress upon me. "I was sure, at any rate," she added, "that he didn't. But he denied certain occasions."

"What occasions?"

"When they had been about together quite as if Quint were his tutor—and a very grand one—and Miss Jessel only for the little lady. When he had gone off with the fellow, I mean, and spent hours with him."

"He then prevaricated about it—he said he hadn't?" Her assent was clear enough to cause me to add in a moment: "I see. He lied."

"Oh!" Mrs. Grose mumbled. This was a suggestion that it didn't matter; which indeed she backed up by a further remark. "You see, after all, Miss Jessel didn't mind. She didn't forbid him."

I considered. "Did he put that to you as a justification?"

At this she dropped again. "No, he never spoke of it."

"Never mentioned her in connection with Quint?"

She saw, visibly flushing, where I was coming out. "Well, he didn't show anything. He denied," she repeated; "he denied."

Lord, how I pressed her now! "So that you could see he knew what was between the two wretches?"

"I don't know—I don't know!" the poor woman groaned.

"You do know, you dear thing," I replied; "only you haven't my dreadful boldness of mind, and you keep back, out of timidity and modesty and delicacy, even the impression that, in the past, when you had, without my aid, to flounder about in silence, most of all made you miserable. But I shall get it out of you yet! There was something in the boy that suggested to you," I continued, "that he covered and concealed their relation."

"Oh, he couldn't prevent—"

"Your learning the truth? I daresay! But, heavens," I fell, with vehemence, athinking, "what it shows that they must, to that extent, have succeeded in making of him!"

Analysis: Notice how James is very careful show Mrs Grose's ambivalence here and the governess's determination to extract a version of events from her which offers little room for doubt. Notice after Mrs Grose offers her "assent" to her comment that Quint spent hours with Miles, the governess now extrapolates that Miles "prevaricated" or been hesitant with Mrs Grose, inferring that Miles lied about being with Quint. We see here how she is now twisting Mrs Grose's account to suit her vision that Miles "concealed" his relation with Quint, while the servant was alive, thus paving the way for her to say that Miles must necessarily conceal his relation with the ghostly Quint. We see how the more dominant, more verbal woman crushes Mrs Grose into accepting her version of events, both past and present. Mrs Grose "groans": the governess interprets this as being an admission that something horrible is going on. But we could see it as Mrs Grose becoming increasingly concerned about the way the governess is pressing her version of events upon her.

Discussion point: What do you think about the way Mrs Grose and the governess is being presented here?

"Ah, nothing that's not nice NOW!" Mrs. Grose lugubriously pleaded.

"I don't wonder you looked queer," I persisted, "when I mentioned to you the letter from his school!"

"I doubt if I looked as queer as you!" she retorted with homely force. "And if he was so bad then as that comes to, how is he such an angel now?"

"Yes, indeed—and if he was a fiend at school! How, how, how? Well," I said in my torment, "you must put it to me again, but I shall not be able to tell you for some days. Only, put it to me again!" I cried in a way that made my friend stare. "There are directions in which I must not for the present let myself go." Meanwhile I returned to her first example—the one to which she had just previously referred—of the boy's happy capacity for an occasional slip. "If Quint—on your remonstrance at the time you speak of—was a base menial, one of the things Miles said to you, I find myself guessing, was that you were another." Again her admission was so adequate that I continued: "And you forgave him that?"

"Wouldn't YOU?"

"Oh, yes!" And we exchanged there, in the stillness, a sound of the oddest amusement. Then I went on: "At all events, while he was with the man—"

"Miss Flora was with the woman. It suited them all!"

It suited me, too, I felt, only too well; by which I mean that it suited exactly the particularly deadly view I was in the very act of forbidding myself to entertain. But I so far succeeded in checking the expression of this view that I will throw, just here, no further light on it than may be offered by the mention of my final observation to Mrs. Grose. "His having lied and been impudent are, I confess, less engaging specimens than I had hoped to have from you of the outbreak in him of the little natural man. Still," I mused, "They must do, for they make me feel more than ever that I must watch."

It made me blush, the next minute, to see in my friend's face how much more unreservedly she had forgiven him than her anecdote struck me as presenting to my own tenderness an occasion for doing. This came out when, at the schoolroom door, she quitted me. "Surely you don't accuse HIM—"

"Of carrying on an intercourse that he conceals from me? Ah, remember that, until further evidence, I now accuse nobody." Then, before shutting her out to go, by another passage, to her own place, "I must just wait," I wound up.

## Questions

What does the governess feel when she returns to the children?

Why does the governess interrogate Mrs Grose?

What does Mrs Grose tell the governess about Miles's misbehavior?

Who was Flora with when Miles was with Quint?

How does Mrs Grose try to defend Miles?

GCSE style question: how James explore the theme of misbehavior in this chapter?

A Level style question: compare and contrast how James explores the theme of corruption of innocence in this story with another relevant text of your choice.

Creative response: write Flora or Miles's diaries for this chapter.

You can find brief answers in the section, **Answers to the Questions**.

# Chapter 9

I waited and waited, and the days, as they elapsed, took something from my consternation. A very few of them, in fact, passing, in constant sight of my pupils, without a fresh incident, sufficed to give to grievous fancies and even to odious memories a kind of brush of the sponge. I have spoken of the surrender to their extraordinary childish grace as a thing I could actively cultivate, and it may be imagined if I neglected now to address myself to this source for whatever it would yield. Stranger than I can express, certainly, was the effort to struggle against my new lights; it would doubtless have been, however, a greater tension still had it not been so frequently successful. I used to wonder how my little charges could help guessing that I thought strange things about them; and the circumstances that these things only made them more interesting was not by itself a direct aid to keeping them in the dark. I trembled lest they should see that they WERE so immensely more interesting. Putting things at the worst, at all events, as in meditation I so often did, any clouding of their innocence could only be—blameless and foredoomed as they were—a reason the more for taking risks. There were moments when, by an irresistible impulse, I found myself catching them up and pressing them to my heart. As soon as I had done so I used to say to myself: "What will they think of that? Doesn't it betray too much?" It would have been easy to get into a sad, wild tangle about how much I might betray; but the real account, I feel, of the hours of peace that I could still enjoy was that the immediate charm of my companions was a beguilement still effective even under the shadow of the possibility that it was studied. For if it occurred to me that I might occasionally excite suspicion by the little outbreaks of my sharper passion for them, so too I remember wondering if I mightn't see a queerness in the traceable increase of their own demonstrations.

They were at this period extravagantly and preternaturally fond of me; which, after all, I could reflect, was no more than a graceful response in children perpetually bowed over and hugged. The homage of which they were so lavish succeeded, in truth, for my nerves, quite as well as if I never appeared to myself, as I may say, literally to catch them at a purpose in it. They had never, I think, wanted to do so many things for their poor protectress; I mean—though they got their lessons better and better, which was naturally what would please her most—in the way of diverting, entertaining, surprising her; reading her passages, telling her stories, acting her charades, pouncing out at her, in disguises, as animals and historical characters, and above all astonishing her by the "pieces" they had secretly got by heart and could interminably recite. I should never get to the bottom—were I to let myself go even now—of the prodigious private commentary, all under still more private correction, with which, in these days, I overscored their full hours. They had shown me from the first a facility for everything, a general faculty which, taking a fresh start, achieved remarkable flights. They got their little tasks as if they loved them, and indulged, from the mere exuberance of the gift, in the most unimposed little miracles of memory. They not only popped out at me as tigers and as Romans, but as Shakespeareans, astronomers, and navigators. This was so singularly the case that it had presumably much to do with the fact as to which, at the present day, I am at a loss for a different explanation: I allude to my unnatural composure on the subject of another school for Miles. What I remember is that I was content not, for the time, to open the question, and that contentment must have sprung from the sense of his perpetually striking show of cleverness. He was too clever for a bad governess, for a parson's daughter, to spoil; and the strangest if not the brightest thread in the pensive embroidery I just spoke of was the impression I might have got, if I had dared to work it out, that he was under some influence operating in his small intellectual life as a tremendous incitement.

If it was easy to reflect, however, that such a boy could postpone school, it was at least as marked that for such a boy to have been "kicked out" by a schoolmaster was a mystification without end. Let me add that in their company now—and I was careful almost never to be out of it—I could follow no scent very far. We lived in a cloud of music and love and success and private theatricals. The musical sense in each of the children was of the quickest, but the elder in especial had a marvelous knack of catching and repeating. The schoolroom piano broke into all gruesome fancies; and when that failed there were confabulations in corners, with a sequel of one of them going out in the highest spirits in order to "come in" as something new. I had had brothers myself, and it was no revelation to me that little girls could be slavish idolaters of little boys. What surpassed everything was that there was a little boy in the world who could have for the inferior age, sex, and intelligence so fine a consideration. They were extraordinarily at one, and to say that they never either quarreled or complained is to make the note of praise coarse for their quality of sweetness. Sometimes, indeed, when I dropped into coarseness, I perhaps came across traces of little understandings between them by which one of them should keep me occupied while the other slipped away. There is a naive side, I suppose, in all diplomacy; but if my pupils practiced upon me, it was surely with the minimum of grossness. It was all in the other quarter that, after a lull, the grossness broke out.

I find that I really hang back; but I must take my plunge. In going on with the record of what was hideous at Bly, I not only challenge the most liberal faith—for which I little care; but—and this is another matter—I renew what I myself suffered, I again push my way through it to the end. There came suddenly an hour after which, as I look back, the affair seems to me to have been all pure suffering; but I have at least reached the heart of it, and the straightest road out is doubtless to advance. One evening—with nothing to lead up or to prepare it—I felt the cold touch of the impression that had breathed on me the night of my arrival and which, much lighter then, as I have mentioned, I should probably have made little of in memory had my subsequent sojourn been less agitated. I had not gone to bed; I sat reading by a couple of candles. There was a roomful of old books at Bly—last-century fiction, some of it, which, to the extent of a distinctly deprecated renown, but never to so much as that of a stray specimen, had reached the sequestered home and appealed to the unavowed curiosity of my youth. I remember that the book I had in my hand was Fielding's Amelia; also that I was wholly awake. I recall further both a general conviction that it was horribly late and a particular objection to looking at my watch. I figure, finally, that the white curtain draping, in the fashion of those days, the head of Flora's little bed, shrouded, as I had assured myself long before, the perfection of childish rest. I recollect in short that, though I was deeply interested in my author, I found myself, at the turn of a page and with his spell all scattered, looking straight up from him and hard at the door of my room. There was a moment during which I listened, reminded of the faint sense I had had, the first night, of there being something undefinably astir in the house, and noted the soft breath of the open casement just move the half-drawn blind. Then, with all the marks of a deliberation that must have seemed magnificent had there been anyone to admire it, I laid down my book, rose to my feet, and, taking a candle, went straight out of the room and, from the passage, on which my light made little impression, noiselessly closed and locked the door.

I can say now neither what determined nor what guided me, but I went straight along the lobby, holding my candle high, till I came within sight of the tall window that presided over the great turn of the staircase. At this point I precipitately found myself aware of three things. They were practically simultaneous, yet they had flashes of succession. My candle, under a bold flourish, went out, and I perceived, by the uncovered window, that the yielding dusk of earliest morning rendered it unnecessary. Without it, the next instant, I saw that there was someone on the stair. I speak of sequences, but I required no lapse of seconds to stiffen myself for a third encounter with Quint. The apparition had reached the landing halfway up and was therefore on the spot nearest the window, where at sight of me, it stopped short and fixed me exactly as it had fixed me from the tower and from the garden. He knew me as well as I knew him; and so, in the cold, faint twilight, with a glimmer in the high glass and another on the polish of the oak stair below, we faced each other in our common intensity. He was absolutely, on this occasion, a living, detestable, dangerous presence.

> **Analysis:** After a lull in events, at night, Quint appears again. This is the first time that a ghost has appeared at night: the atmosphere is very Gothic and deliberately spooky. What is fascinating is that despite the candle being put out, the governess is very brave, not worried at all. Far from it, she says: "we faced each other in our common intensity". This is a magnetic description: the two of them seem both attracted and repelled by each other. She describes him as "living" presence: he has physicality for her. The alliteration of "detestable" and "dangerous" draws attention to the governess's contradictory feelings towards Quint: both hatred, but also an awareness that his living presence is thrillingly exciting as only a dangerous person can be.

> **Discussion point:** How does James build suspense at this point? In what ways is this part of the novel like a traditional ghost story, and in what ways does it differ?

But that was not the wonder of wonders; I reserve this distinction for quite another circumstance: the circumstance that dread had unmistakably quitted me and that there was nothing in me there that didn't meet and measure him.

I had plenty of anguish after that extraordinary moment, but I had, thank God, no terror. And he knew I had not—I found myself at the end of an instant magnificently aware of this. I felt, in a fierce rigor of confidence, that if I stood my ground a minute I should cease—for the time, at least—to have him to reckon with; and during the minute, accordingly, the thing was as human and hideous as a real interview: hideous just because it WAS human, as human as to have met alone, in the small hours, in a sleeping house, some enemy, some adventurer, some criminal. It was the dead silence of our long gaze at such close quarters that gave the whole horror, huge as it was, its only note of the unnatural. If I had met a murderer in such a place and at such an hour, we still at least would have spoken. Something would have passed, in life, between us; if nothing had passed, one of us would have moved. The moment was so prolonged that it would have taken but little more to make me doubt if even I were in life. I can't express what followed it save by saying that the silence itself—which was indeed in a manner an attestation of my strength—became the element into which I saw the figure disappear; in which I definitely saw it turn as I might have seen the low wretch to which it had once belonged turn on receipt of an order, and pass, with my eyes on the villainous back that no hunch could have more disfigured, straight down the staircase and into the darkness in which the next bend was lost.

### Questions

How does the governess's relationship with the children progress?
Why does the governess think the children are possibly being nice?
What happens one night when the governess is startled while reading? What does she do and see?
What does the governess do when she sees Quint?
GCSE style question: How does James make the sighting of Quint on the stairway so haunting?
A Level style question: examining another relevant text of your choice, compare and contrast an atmospheric scene set at night-time with the one in this chapter.
Creative response: write a description of someone who sees a ghost in the night.
Creative response: write a monologue spoken by Peter Quint.
You can find brief answers in the section, **Answers to the Questions**.

# Chapter 10

I remained awhile at the top of the stair, but with the effect presently of understanding that when my visitor had gone, he had gone: then I returned to my room. The foremost thing I saw there by the light of the candle I had left burning was that Flora's little bed was empty; and on this I caught my breath with all the terror that, five minutes before, I had been able to resist. I dashed at the place in which I had left her lying and over which (for the small silk counterpane and the sheets were disarranged) the white curtains had been deceivingly pulled forward; then my step, to my unutterable relief, produced an answering sound: I perceived an agitation of the window blind, and the child, ducking down, emerged rosily from the other side of it. She stood there in so much of her candor and so little of her nightgown, with her pink bare feet and the golden glow of her curls. She looked intensely grave, and I had never had such a sense of losing an advantage acquired (the thrill of which had just been so prodigious) as on my consciousness that she addressed me with a reproach. "You naughty: where HAVE you been?"—instead of challenging her own irregularity I found myself arraigned and explaining. She herself explained, for that matter, with the loveliest, eagerest simplicity. She had known suddenly, as she lay there, that I was out of the room, and had jumped up to see what had become of me. I had dropped, with the joy of her reappearance, back into my chair—feeling then, and then only, a little faint; and she had pattered straight over to me, thrown herself upon my knee, given herself to be held with the flame of the candle full in the wonderful little face that was still flushed with sleep. I remember closing my eyes an instant, yieldingly, consciously, as before the excess of something beautiful that shone out of the blue of her own. "You were looking for me out of the window?" I said. "You thought I might be walking in the grounds?"

"Well, you know, I thought someone was"—she never blanched as she smiled out that at me.

Oh, how I looked at her now! "And did you see anyone?"

"Ah, NO!" she returned, almost with the full privilege of childish inconsequence, resentfully, though with a long sweetness in her little drawl of the negative.

At that moment, in the state of my nerves, I absolutely believed she lied; and if I once more closed my eyes it was before the dazzle of the three or four possible ways in which I might take this up. One of these, for a moment, tempted me with such singular intensity that, to withstand it, I must have gripped my little girl with a spasm that, wonderfully, she submitted to without a cry or a sign of fright. Why not break out at her on the spot and have it all over?—give it to her straight in her lovely little lighted face? "You see, you see, you KNOW that you do and that you already quite suspect I believe it; therefore, why not frankly confess it to me, so that we may at least live with it together and learn perhaps, in the strangeness of our fate, where we are and what it means?" This solicitation dropped, alas, as it came: if I could immediately have succumbed to it I might have spared myself—well, you'll see what. Instead of succumbing I sprang again to my feet, looked at her bed, and took a helpless middle way. "Why did you pull the curtain over the place to make me think you were still there?"

Flora luminously considered; after which, with her little divine smile: "Because I don't like to frighten you!"

"But if I had, by your idea, gone out—?"

She absolutely declined to be puzzled; she turned her eyes to the flame of the candle as if the question were as irrelevant, or at any rate as impersonal, as Mrs. Marcet or nine-times-nine. "Oh, but you know," she quite adequately answered, "that you might come back, you dear, and that you HAVE!" And after a little, when she had got into bed, I had, for a long time, by almost sitting on her to hold her hand, to prove that I recognized the pertinence of my return.

You may imagine the general complexion, from that moment, of my nights. I repeatedly sat up till I didn't know when; I selected moments when my roommate unmistakably slept, and, stealing out, took noiseless turns in the passage and even pushed as far as to where I had last met Quint. But I never met him there again; and I may as well say at once that I on no other occasion saw him in the house. I just missed, on the staircase, on the other hand, a different adventure. Looking down it from the top I once recognized the presence of a woman seated on one of the lower steps with her back presented to me, her body half-bowed and her head, in an attitude of woe, in her hands. I had been there but an instant, however, when she vanished without looking round at me. I knew, nonetheless, exactly what dreadful face she had to show; and I wondered whether, if instead of being above I had been below, I should have had, for going up, the same nerve I had lately shown Quint. Well, there continued to be plenty of chance for nerve. On the eleventh night after my latest encounter with that gentleman—they were all numbered now—I had an alarm that perilously skirted it and that indeed, from the particular quality of its unexpectedness, proved quite my sharpest shock. It was precisely the first night during this series that, weary with watching, I had felt that I might again without laxity lay myself down at my old hour. I slept immediately and, as I afterward knew, till about one o'clock; but when I woke it was to sit straight up, as completely roused as if a hand had shook me. I had left a light burning, but it was now out, and I felt an instant certainty that Flora had extinguished it. This brought me to my feet and straight, in the darkness, to her bed, which I found she had left. A glance at the window enlightened me further, and the striking of a match completed the picture.

The child had again got up—this time blowing out the taper, and had again, for some purpose of observation or response, squeezed in behind the blind and was peering out into the night. That she now saw—as she had not, I had satisfied myself, the previous time—was proved to me by the fact that she was disturbed neither by my reillumination nor by the haste I made to get into slippers and into a wrap. Hidden, protected, absorbed, she evidently rested on the sill—the casement opened forward—and gave herself up. There was a great still moon to help her, and this fact had counted in my quick decision. She was face to face with the apparition we had met at the lake, and could now communicate with it as she had not then been able to do. What I, on my side, had to care for was, without disturbing her, to reach, from the corridor, some other window in the same quarter. I got to the door without her hearing me; I got out of it, closed it, and listened, from the other side, for some sound from her. While I stood in the passage I had my eyes on her brother's door, which was but ten steps off and which, indescribably, produced in me a renewal of the strange impulse that I lately spoke of as my temptation. What if I should go straight in and march to HIS window?—what if, by risking to his boyish bewilderment a revelation of my motive, I should throw across the rest of the mystery the long halter of my boldness?

This thought held me sufficiently to make me cross to his threshold and pause again. I preternaturally listened; I figured to myself what might portentously be; I wondered if his bed were also empty and he too were secretly at watch. It was a deep, soundless minute, at the end of which my impulse failed. He was quiet; he might be innocent; the risk was hideous; I turned away. There was a figure in the grounds—a figure prowling for a sight, the visitor with whom Flora was engaged; but it was not the visitor most concerned with my boy. I hesitated afresh, but on other grounds and only for a few seconds; then I had made my choice. There were empty rooms at Bly, and it was only a question of choosing the right one. The right one suddenly presented itself to me as the lower one—though high above the gardens—in the solid corner of the house that I have spoken of as the old tower. This was a large, square chamber, arranged with some state as a bedroom, the extravagant size of which made it so inconvenient that it had not for years, though kept by Mrs. Grose in exemplary order, been occupied. I had often admired it and I knew my way about in it; I had only, after just faltering at the first chill gloom of its disuse, to pass across it and unbolt as quietly as I could one of the shutters. Achieving this transit, I uncovered the glass without a sound and, applying my face to the pane, was able, the darkness without being much less than within, to see that I commanded the right direction. Then I saw something more. The moon made the night extraordinarily penetrable and showed me on the lawn a person, diminished by distance, who stood there motionless and as if fascinated, looking up to where I had appeared—looking, that is, not so much straight at me as at something that was apparently above me. There was clearly another person above me—there was a person on the tower; but the presence on the lawn was not in the least what I had conceived and had confidently hurried to meet. The presence on the lawn—I felt sick as I made it out—was poor little Miles himself.

Analysis: James has carefully built up to this moment. Before it, on the night that her candle was extinguished and she saw Quint on the stairs, she found Flora out of her bed and hiding behind a curtain, but not willing to explain why. Now discovering Flora by the window but careful not to disturb her, the governess sees Miles standing on the lawn apparently looking Quint who is standing above her. Notice how skilful James' description is: it is a very haunting, supernatural description of children conversing with ghosts on one hand -- if we believe the governess -- but from another perspective, read the description very carefully, and you realise it proves very little, except that the children are out of their beds, clearly disturbed and upset.

Discussion point: What evidence is there that Miles and Flora are communicating with the ghosts? What evidence is there that they are not?

## Questions

Where does the governess find Flora and why does it trouble her?

Why does the governess find it difficult to sleep after this incident?

What happens when the governess finally decides to go to bed at the normal time?

Where does she find the children? What does she think Flora is doing?

GCSE style question: how does make the governess's uncertainty and confusion so suspenseful in this chapter?

A Level style question: compare and contrast James's representation of Flora with another representation of a little girl in a relevant text of your choice.

Creative response: write diary entries for Flora and Miles for this chapter.

You can find brief answers in the section, **Answers to the Questions**.

# Chapter 11

It was not till late next day that I spoke to Mrs. Grose; the rigor with which I kept my pupils in sight making it often difficult to meet her privately, and the more as we each felt the importance of not provoking—on the part of the servants quite as much as on that of the children—any suspicion of a secret flurry or that of a discussion of mysteries. I drew a great security in this particular from her mere smooth aspect. There was nothing in her fresh face to pass on to others my horrible confidences. She believed me, I was sure, absolutely: if she hadn't I don't know what would have become of me, for I couldn't have borne the business alone. But she was a magnificent monument to the blessing of a want of imagination, and if she could see in our little charges nothing but their beauty and amiability, their happiness and cleverness, she had no direct communication with the sources of my trouble. If they had been at all visibly blighted or battered, she would doubtless have grown, on tracing it back, haggard enough to match them; as matters stood, however, I could feel her, when she surveyed them, with her large white arms folded and the habit of serenity in all her look, thank the Lord's mercy that if they were ruined the pieces would still serve. Flights of fancy gave place, in her mind, to a steady fireside glow, and I had already begun to perceive how, with the development of the conviction that—as time went on without a public accident—our young things could, after all, look out for themselves, she addressed her greatest solicitude to the sad case presented by their instructress. That, for myself, was a sound simplification: I could engage that, to the world, my face should tell no tales, but it would have been, in the conditions, an immense added strain to find myself anxious about hers.

At the hour I now speak of she had joined me, under pressure, on the terrace, where, with the lapse of the season, the afternoon sun was now agreeable; and we sat there together while, before us, at a distance, but within call if we wished, the children strolled to and fro in one of their most manageable moods. They moved slowly, in unison, below us, over the lawn, the boy, as they went, reading aloud from a storybook and passing his arm round his sister to keep her quite in touch. Mrs. Grose watched them with positive placidity; then I caught the suppressed intellectual creak with which she conscientiously turned to take from me a view of the back of the tapestry. I had made her a receptacle of lurid things, but there was an odd recognition of my superiority—my accomplishments and my function—in her patience under my pain. She offered her mind to my disclosures as, had I wished to mix a witch's broth and proposed it with assurance, she would have held out a large clean saucepan. This had become thoroughly her attitude by the time that, in my recital of the events of the night, I reached the point of what Miles had said to me when, after seeing him, at such a monstrous hour, almost on the very spot where he happened now to be, I had gone down to bring him in; choosing then, at the window, with a concentrated need of not alarming the house, rather that method than a signal more resonant. I had left her meanwhile in little doubt of my small hope of representing with success even to her actual sympathy my sense of the real splendor of the little inspiration with which, after I had got him into the house, the boy met my final articulate challenge. As soon as I appeared in the moonlight on the terrace, he had come to me as straight as possible; on which I had taken his hand without a word and led him, through the dark spaces, up the staircase where Quint had so hungrily hovered for him, along the lobby where I had listened and trembled, and so to his forsaken room.

Not a sound, on the way, had passed between us, and I had wondered—oh, HOW I had wondered!—if he were groping about in his little mind for something plausible and not too grotesque. It would tax his invention, certainly, and I felt, this time, over his real embarrassment, a curious thrill of triumph. It was a sharp trap for the inscrutable! He couldn't play any longer at innocence; so how the deuce would he get out of it? There beat in me indeed, with the passionate throb of this question an equal dumb appeal as to how the deuce I should. I was confronted at last, as never yet, with all the risk attached even now to sounding my own horrid note. I remember in fact that as we pushed into his little chamber, where the bed had not been slept in at all and the window, uncovered to the moonlight, made the place so clear that there was no need of striking a match—I remember how I suddenly dropped, sank upon the edge of the bed from the force of the idea that he must know how he really, as they say, "had" me. He could do what he liked, with all his cleverness to help him, so long as I should continue to defer to the old tradition of the criminality of those caretakers of the young who minister to superstitions and fears. He "had" me indeed, and in a cleft stick; for who would ever absolve me, who would consent that I should go unhung, if, by the faintest tremor of an overture, I were the first to introduce into our perfect intercourse an element so dire? No, no: it was useless to attempt to convey to Mrs. Grose, just as it is scarcely less so to attempt to suggest here, how, in our short, stiff brush in the dark, he fairly shook me with admiration. I was of course thoroughly kind and merciful; never, never yet had I placed on his little shoulders hands of such tenderness as those with which, while I rested against the bed, I held him there well under fire. I had no alternative but, in form at least, to put it to him.

"You must tell me now—and all the truth. What did you go out for? What were you doing there?"

I can still see his wonderful smile, the whites of his beautiful eyes, and the uncovering of his little teeth shine to me in the dusk. "If I tell you why, will you understand?" My heart, at this, leaped into my mouth. WOULD he tell me why? I found no sound on my lips to press it, and I was aware of replying only with a vague, repeated, grimacing nod. He was gentleness itself, and while I wagged my head at him he stood there more than ever a little fairy prince. It was his brightness indeed that gave me a respite. Would it be so great if he were really going to tell me? "Well," he said at last, "just exactly in order that you should do this."

"Do what?"

"Think me—for a change—BAD!" I shall never forget the sweetness and gaiety with which he brought out the word, nor how, on top of it, he bent forward and kissed me. It was practically the end of everything. I met his kiss and I had to make, while I folded him for a minute in my arms, the most stupendous effort not to cry. He had given exactly the account of himself that permitted least of my going behind it, and it was only with the effect of confirming my acceptance of it that, as I presently glanced about the room, I could say—

"Then you didn't undress at all?"

He fairly glittered in the gloom. "Not at all. I sat up and read."

"And when did you go down?"

"At midnight. When I'm bad I AM bad!"

"I see, I see—it's charming. But how could you be sure I would know it?"

"Oh, I arranged that with Flora." His answers rang out with a readiness! "She was to get up and look out."

"Which is what she did do." It was I who fell into the trap!

"So she disturbed you, and, to see what she was looking at, you also looked—you saw."

"While you," I concurred, "caught your death in the night air!"

He literally bloomed so from this exploit that he could afford radiantly to assent. "How otherwise should I have been bad enough?" he asked. Then, after another embrace, the incident and our interview closed on my recognition of all the reserves of goodness that, for his joke, he had been able to draw upon.

> Analysis: Here we see James developing one of the central themes in his work; the adult world's perception of children. The nurse describes Miles as glittering in the "gloom". In other words, Miles is triumphant about his being able to converse with the ghosts and do what he wants, disobeying her orders. Notice also how there is ambiguity about the use of pronouns here: "She was get up and look out." This most obviously refers to Flora, but, if we believe that

the children are in league with the ghosts, it could also refer to Miss Jessel. There is another interpretation about Miles' behaviour: that he is not league with the ghosts at all, but wishes to defy the controlling governess; he seems to enjoy the thought of being "bad". Here there is a poignancy about Miles, the serious, isolated, sickly boy, who yearns to be likely ordinary boys; to do daring things. The governess doesn't seem to be able to be cross with him: she embraces him.

Discussion point: What do you think Miles means when he says he was being "bad"?

## Questions

What does the governess tell Mrs Grose the next morning?

How does the governess respond to Miles's story about being bad?

GCSE style question: how does James create a narrative twist in this chapter?

Creative response: write Mrs Grose's diary for this chapter, exploring her thoughts and feelings about what the governess has said.

You can find brief answers in the section, **Answers to the Questions**.

# Chapter 12

The particular impression I had received proved in the morning light, I repeat, not quite successfully presentable to Mrs. Grose, though I reinforced it with the mention of still another remark that he had made before we separated. "It all lies in half a dozen words," I said to her, "words that really settle the matter. 'Think, you know, what I MIGHT do!' He threw that off to show me how good he is. He knows down to the ground what he 'might' do. That's what he gave them a taste of at school."

"Lord, you do change!" cried my friend.

"I don't change—I simply make it out. The four, depend upon it, perpetually meet. If on either of these last nights you had been with either child, you would clearly have understood. The more I've watched and waited the more I've felt that if there were nothing else to make it sure it would be made so by the systematic silence of each. NEVER, by a slip of the tongue, have they so much as alluded to either of their old friends, any more than Miles has alluded to his expulsion. Oh, yes, we may sit here and look at them, and they may show off to us there to their fill; but even while they pretend to be lost in their fairytale they're steeped in their vision of the dead restored. He's not reading to her," I declared; "they're talking of THEM—they're talking horrors! I go on, I know, as if I were crazy; and it's a wonder I'm not. What I've seen would have made YOU so; but it has only made me more lucid, made me get hold of still other things."

My lucidity must have seemed awful, but the charming creatures who were victims of it, passing and repassing in their interlocked sweetness, gave my colleague something to hold on by; and I felt how tight she held as, without stirring in the breath of my passion, she covered them still with her eyes. "Of what other things have you got hold?"

"Why, of the very things that have delighted, fascinated, and yet, at bottom, as I now so strangely see, mystified and troubled me. Their more than earthly beauty, their absolutely unnatural goodness. It's a game," I went on; "it's a policy and a fraud!"

"On the part of little darlings—?"

"As yet mere lovely babies? Yes, mad as that seems!" The very act of bringing it out really helped me to trace it—follow it all up and piece it all together. "They haven't been good—they've only been absent. It has been easy to live with them, because they're simply leading a life of their own. They're not mine—they're not ours. They're his and they're hers!"

"Quint's and that woman's?"

"Quint's and that woman's. They want to get to them."

Oh, how, at this, poor Mrs. Grose appeared to study them! "But for what?"

Analysis: Here we see the governess developing her theory about the children, looking back upon her whole time with them and seeing it as a "policy and a fraud". In other words, they've been in league with the ghosts all this time and have only been pretending to be good. Here, we see Mrs Grose's questions become even more disbelieving.

Discussion point: Mrs Grose's question is a good one. If the ghosts are real, what do they want to get from the children?

"For the love of all the evil that, in those dreadful days, the pair put into them. And to ply them with that evil still, to keep up the work of demons, is what brings the others back."

"Laws!" said my friend under her breath. The exclamation was homely, but it revealed a real acceptance of my further proof of what, in the bad time—for there had been a worse even than this!—must have occurred. There could have been no such justification for me as the plain assent of her experience to whatever depth of depravity I found credible in our brace of scoundrels. It was in obvious submission of memory that she brought out after a moment: "They WERE rascals! But what can they now do?" she pursued.

"Do?" I echoed so loud that Miles and Flora, as they passed at their distance, paused an instant in their walk and looked at us. "Don't they do enough?" I demanded in a lower tone, while the children, having smiled and nodded and kissed hands to us, resumed their exhibition. We were held by it a minute; then I answered: "They can destroy them!" At this my companion did turn, but the inquiry she launched was a silent one, the effect of which was to make me more explicit. "They don't know, as yet, quite how—but they're trying hard. They're seen only across, as it were, and beyond—in strange places and on high places, the top of towers, the roof of houses, the outside of windows, the further edge of pools; but there's a deep design, on either side, to shorten the distance and overcome the obstacle; and the success of the tempters is only a question of time. They've only to keep to their suggestions of danger."

"For the children to come?"

"And perish in the attempt!" Mrs. Grose slowly got up, and I scrupulously added: "Unless, of course, we can prevent!"

Standing there before me while I kept my seat, she visibly turned things over. "Their uncle must do the preventing. He must take them away."

"And who's to make him?"

She had been scanning the distance, but she now dropped on me a foolish face. "You, miss."

"By writing to him that his house is poisoned and his little nephew and niece mad?"

"But if they ARE, miss?"

"And if I am myself, you mean? That's charming news to be sent him by a governess whose prime undertaking was to give him no worry."

Mrs. Grose considered, following the children again. "Yes, he do hate worry. That was the great reason—"

"Why those fiends took him in so long? No doubt, though his indifference must have been awful. As I'm not a fiend, at any rate, I shouldn't take him in."

My companion, after an instant and for all answer, sat down again and grasped my arm. "Make him at any rate come to you."

I stared. "To ME?" I had a sudden fear of what she might do. "'Him'?"

"He ought to BE here—he ought to help."

I quickly rose, and I think I must have shown her a queerer face than ever yet. "You see me asking him for a visit?" No, with her eyes on my face she evidently couldn't. Instead of it even—as a woman reads another—she could see what I myself saw: his derision, his amusement, his contempt for the breakdown of my resignation at being left alone and for the fine machinery I had set in motion to attract his attention to my slighted charms. She didn't know—no one knew—how proud I had been to serve him and to stick to our terms; yet she nonetheless took the measure, I think, of the warning I now gave her. "If you should so lose your head as to appeal to him for me—"

She was really frightened. "Yes, miss?"

"I would leave, on the spot, both him and you."

## Questions

What does the governess tell Mrs Grose about what she really thinks the children are up to?

What does the governess think Quint and Miss Jessel are planning?

What are Mrs Grose's suggestions? What is the governess's response?

GCSE style question: how does James develop the character of the governess and Mrs Grose in this chapter?

A Level style question: compare and contrast the way in which James represents evil in this story with the representation of evil in another relevant text of your choice.

Creative response: write Mrs Grose's diary for this chapter.

Creative response: write a story called 'The Evil Child'.

You can find brief answers in the section, **Answers to the Questions**.

# Chapter 13

It was all very well to join them, but speaking to them proved quite as much as ever an effort beyond my strength—offered, in close quarters, difficulties as insurmountable as before. This situation continued a month, and with new aggravations and particular notes, the note above all, sharper and sharper, of the small ironic consciousness on the part of my pupils. It was not, I am as sure today as I was sure then, my mere infernal imagination: it was absolutely traceable that they were aware of my predicament and that this strange relation made, in a manner, for a long time, the air in which we moved. I don't mean that they had their tongues in their cheeks or did anything vulgar, for that was not one of their dangers: I do mean, on the other hand, that the element of the unnamed and untouched became, between us, greater than any other, and that so much avoidance could not have been so successfully effected without a great deal of tacit arrangement. It was as if, at moments, we were perpetually coming into sight of subjects before which we must stop short, turning suddenly out of alleys that we perceived to be blind, closing with a little bang that made us look at each other—for, like all bangs, it was something louder than we had intended—the doors we had indiscreetly opened. All roads lead to Rome, and there were times when it might have struck us that almost every branch of study or subject of conversation skirted forbidden ground. Forbidden ground was the question of the return of the dead in general and of whatever, in especial, might survive, in memory, of the friends little children had lost. There were days when I could have sworn that one of them had, with a small invisible nudge, said to the other: "She thinks she'll do it this time—but she WON'T!" To "do it" would have been to indulge for instance—and for once in a way—in some direct reference to the lady who had prepared them for my discipline. They had a delightful endless appetite for passages in my own history, to which I had again and again treated them; they were in possession of everything that had ever happened to me, had had, with every circumstance the story of my smallest adventures and of those of my brothers and sisters and of the cat and the dog at home, as well as many particulars of the eccentric nature of my father, of the furniture and arrangement of our house, and of the conversation of the old women of our village. There were things enough, taking one with another, to chatter about, if one went very fast and knew by instinct when to go round. They pulled with an art of their own the strings of my invention and my memory; and nothing else perhaps, when I thought of such occasions afterward, gave me so the suspicion of being watched from under cover. It was in any case over MY life, MY past, and MY friends alone that we could take anything like our ease—a state of affairs that led them sometimes without the least pertinence to break out into sociable reminders. I was invited—with no visible connection—to repeat afresh Goody Gosling's celebrated mot or to confirm the details already supplied as to the cleverness of the vicarage pony.

It was partly at such junctures as these and partly at quite different ones that, with the turn my matters had now taken, my predicament, as I have called it, grew most sensible. The fact that the days passed for me without another encounter ought, it would have appeared, to have done something toward soothing my nerves. Since the light brush, that second night on the upper landing, of the presence of a woman at the foot of the stair, I had seen nothing, whether in or out of the house, that one had better not have seen. There was many a corner round which I expected to come upon Quint, and many a situation that, in a merely sinister way, would have favored the appearance of Miss Jessel. The summer had turned, the summer had gone; the autumn had dropped upon Bly and had blown out half our lights. The place, with its gray sky and withered garlands, its bared spaces and scattered dead leaves, was like a theater after the performance— all strewn with crumpled playbills. There were exactly states of the air, conditions of sound and of stillness, unspeakable impressions of the KIND of ministering moment, that brought back to me, long enough to catch it, the feeling of the medium in which, that June evening out of doors, I had had my first sight of Quint, and in which, too, at those other instants, I had, after seeing him through the window, looked for him in vain in the circle of shrubbery. I recognized the signs, the portents—I recognized the moment, the spot. But they remained unaccompanied and empty, and I continued unmolested; if unmolested one could call a young woman whose sensibility had, in the most extraordinary fashion, not declined but deepened. I had said in my talk with Mrs. Grose on that horrid scene of Flora's by the lake— and had perplexed her by so saying—that it would from that moment distress me much more to lose my power than to keep it. I had then expressed what was vividly in my mind: the truth that, whether the children really saw or not—since, that is, it was not yet definitely proved—I greatly preferred, as a safeguard, the fullness of my own exposure. I was ready to know the very worst that was to be known. What I had then had an ugly glimpse of was that my eyes might be sealed just while theirs were most opened. Well, my eyes WERE sealed, it appeared, at present—a consummation for which it seemed blasphemous not to thank God. There was, alas, a difficulty about that: I would have thanked him with all my soul had I not had in a proportionate measure this conviction of the secret of my pupils.

How can I retrace today the strange steps of my obsession? There were times of our being together when I would have been ready to swear that, literally, in my presence, but with my direct sense of it closed, they had visitors who were known and were welcome. Then it was that, had I not been deterred by the very chance that such an injury might prove greater than the injury to be averted, my exultation would have broken out. "They're here, they're here, you little wretches," I would have cried, "and you can't deny it now!" The little wretches denied it with all the added volume of their sociability and their tenderness, in just the crystal depths of which—like the flash of a fish in a stream—the mockery of their advantage peeped up. The shock, in truth, had sunk into me still deeper than I knew on the night when, looking out to see either Quint or Miss Jessel under the stars, I had beheld the boy over whose rest I watched and who had immediately brought in with him—had straightway, there, turned it on me—the lovely upward look with which, from the battlements above me, the hideous apparition of Quint had played. If it was a question of a scare, my discovery on this occasion had scared me more than any other, and it was in the condition of nerves produced by it that I made my actual inductions. They harassed me so that sometimes, at odd moments, I shut myself up audibly to rehearse—it was at once a fantastic relief and a renewed despair—the manner in which I might come to the point. I approached it from one side and the other while, in my room, I flung myself about, but I always broke down in the monstrous utterance of names. As they died away on my lips, I said to myself that I should indeed help them to represent something infamous, if, by pronouncing them, I should violate as rare a little case of instinctive delicacy as any schoolroom, probably, had ever known. When I said to myself: "THEY have the manners to be silent, and you, trusted as you are, the baseness to speak!" I felt myself crimson and I covered my face with my hands. After these secret scenes I chattered more than ever, going on volubly enough till one of our prodigious, palpable hushes occurred—I can call them nothing else—the strange, dizzy lift or swim (I try for terms!) into a stillness, a pause of all life, that had nothing to do with the more or less noise that at the moment we might be engaged in making and that I could hear through any deepened exhilaration or quickened recitation or louder strum of the piano. Then it was that the others, the outsiders, were there. Though they were not angels, they "passed," as the French say, causing me, while they stayed, to tremble with the fear of their addressing to their younger victims some yet more infernal message or more vivid image than they had thought good enough for myself.

What it was most impossible to get rid of was the cruel idea that, whatever I had seen, Miles and Flora saw MORE—things terrible and unguessable and that sprang from dreadful passages of intercourse in the past. Such things naturally left on the surface, for the time, a chill which we vociferously denied that we felt; and we had, all three, with repetition, got into such splendid training that we went, each time, almost automatically, to mark the close of the incident, through the very same movements. It was striking of the children, at all events, to kiss me inveterately with a kind of wild irrelevance and never to fail—one or the other—of the precious question that had helped us through many a peril.

Analysis: Here we see the governess's paranoia develop and spread, invading her every interaction with them. Every dealing with them now has a sinister edge and undertone to them: the children's affection is merely a fraud. Their kisses are there merely to distract her from asking questions about the ghosts.

Discussion point: Is the governess descending into a form of madness here or is she seeing the truth?

"When do you think he WILL come? Don't you think we OUGHT to write?"—there was nothing like that inquiry, we found by experience, for carrying off an awkwardness. "He" of course was their uncle in Harley Street; and we lived in much profusion of theory that he might at any moment arrive to mingle in our circle. It was impossible to have given less encouragement than he had done to such a doctrine, but if we had not had the doctrine to fall back upon we should have deprived each other of some of our finest exhibitions. He never wrote to them—that may have been selfish, but it was a part of the flattery of his trust of me; for the way in which a man pays his highest tribute to a woman is apt to be but by the more festal celebration of one of the sacred laws of his comfort; and I held that I carried out the spirit of the pledge given not to appeal to him when I let my charges understand that their own letters were but charming literary exercises. They were too beautiful to be posted; I kept them myself; I have them all to this hour. This was a rule indeed which only added to the satiric effect of my being plied with the supposition that he might at any moment be among us. It was exactly as if my charges knew how almost more awkward than anything else that might be for me. There appears to me, moreover, as I look back, no note in all this more extraordinary than the mere fact that, in spite of my tension and of their triumph, I never lost patience with them. Adorable they must in truth have been, I now reflect, that I didn't in these days hate them! Would exasperation, however, if relief had longer been postponed, finally have betrayed me? It little matters, for relief arrived. I call it relief, though it was only the relief that a snap brings to a strain or the burst of a thunderstorm to a day of suffocation. It was at least change, and it came with a rush.

## Questions

What does the governess think the children know? What is her evidence for this?

As time passes, what does the governess think the children might be doing?

Why does the governess shut herself away?

What do the children ask her about?

What does the governess suggest they do?

GCSE style question: how does James create a sense of psychological horror in this chapter?

A Level style question: compare and contrast this story with another text that conjures an atmosphere of psychological horror.

Creative response: write Miles and/or Flora's diary entries for this chapter.

You can find brief answers in the section, **Answers to the Questions**.

# Chapter 14

Walking to church a certain Sunday morning, I had little Miles at my side and his sister, in advance of us and at Mrs. Grose's, well in sight. It was a crisp, clear day, the first of its order for some time; the night had brought a touch of frost, and the autumn air, bright and sharp, made the church bells almost gay. It was an odd accident of thought that I should have happened at such a moment to be particularly and very gratefully struck with the obedience of my little charges. Why did they never resent my inexorable, my perpetual society? Something or other had brought nearer home to me that I had all but pinned the boy to my shawl and that, in the way our companions were marshaled before me, I might have appeared to provide against some danger of rebellion. I was like a gaoler with an eye to possible surprises and escapes. But all this belonged—I mean their magnificent little surrender—just to the special array of the facts that were most abysmal. Turned out for Sunday by his uncle's tailor, who had had a free hand and a notion of pretty waistcoats and of his grand little air, Miles's whole title to independence, the rights of his sex and situation, were so stamped upon him that if he had suddenly struck for freedom I should have had nothing to say. I was by the strangest of chances wondering how I should meet him when the revolution unmistakably occurred. I call it a revolution because I now see how, with the word he spoke, the curtain rose on the last act of my dreadful drama, and the catastrophe was precipitated. "Look here, my dear, you know," he charmingly said, "when in the world, please, am I going back to school?"

Transcribed here the speech sounds harmless enough, particularly as uttered in the sweet, high, casual pipe with which, at all interlocutors, but above all at his eternal governess, he threw off intonations as if he were tossing roses. There was something in them that always made one "catch," and I caught, at any rate, now so effectually that I stopped as short as if one of the trees of the park had fallen across the road. There was something new, on the spot, between us, and he was perfectly aware that I recognized it, though, to enable me to do so, he had no need to look a whit less candid and charming than usual. I could feel in him how he already, from my at first finding nothing to reply, perceived the advantage he had gained. I was so slow to find anything that he had plenty of time, after a minute, to continue with his suggestive but inconclusive smile: "You know, my dear, that for a fellow to be with a lady ALWAYS—!" His "my dear" was constantly on his lips for me, and nothing could have expressed more the exact shade of the sentiment with which I desired to inspire my pupils than its fond familiarity. It was so respectfully easy.

But, oh, how I felt that at present I must pick my own phrases! I remember that, to gain time, I tried to laugh, and I seemed to see in the beautiful face with which he watched me how ugly and queer I looked. "And always with the same lady?" I returned.

## Analysis: We now realise that Miles wishes to be away from the cloying, over-protective, over-affectionate presence of the governess and to be back at school. We gain a sense that Miles wishes to be amidst more masculine company. He says: "for a fellow to be with a lady *always* – !" There are obviously two reasons why he might want to be away from her: either because she knows the truth about the ghosts, or because she's becoming over-protective, mothering him too much. Now we see Miles really standing up to the governess: he asks to go back to school and for his uncle to come to Bly. He craves male company. Mrs Grose has already advised the governess to write to her employer, asking him to intervene, but she has refused, not wanting to bother him and show that she is dependent upon him. She wants to feel that she is in control of the situation.

## Discussion point: What are the advantages and disadvantages of boys being very close to one female teacher when they are nine years old like Miles?

He neither blanched nor winked. The whole thing was virtually out between us. "Ah, of course, she's a jolly, 'perfect' lady; but, after all, I'm a fellow, don't you see? that's—well, getting on."

I lingered there with him an instant ever so kindly. "Yes, you're getting on." Oh, but I felt helpless!

I have kept to this day the heartbreaking little idea of how he seemed to know that and to play with it. "And you can't say I've not been awfully good, can you?"

I laid my hand on his shoulder, for, though I felt how much better it would have been to walk on, I was not yet quite able. "No, I can't say that, Miles."

"Except just that one night, you know—!"

"That one night?" I couldn't look as straight as he.

"Why, when I went down—went out of the house."

"Oh, yes. But I forget what you did it for."

"You forget?"—he spoke with the sweet extravagance of childish reproach. "Why, it was to show you I could!"

"Oh, yes, you could."

"And I can again."

I felt that I might, perhaps, after all, succeed in keeping my wits about me. "Certainly. But you won't."

"No, not THAT again. It was nothing."

"It was nothing," I said. "But we must go on."

He resumed our walk with me, passing his hand into my arm. "Then when AM I going back?"

I wore, in turning it over, my most responsible air. "Were you very happy at school?"

He just considered. "Oh, I'm happy enough anywhere!"

"Well, then," I quavered, "if you're just as happy here—!"

"Ah, but that isn't everything! Of course YOU know a lot—"

"But you hint that you know almost as much?" I risked as he paused.

"Not half I want to!" Miles honestly professed. "But it isn't so much that."

"What is it, then?"

"Well—I want to see more life."

"I see; I see." We had arrived within sight of the church and of various persons, including several of the household of Bly, on their way to it and clustered about the door to see us go in. I quickened our step; I wanted to get there before the question between us opened up much further; I reflected hungrily that, for more than an hour, he would have to be silent; and I thought with envy of the comparative dusk of the pew and of the almost spiritual help of the hassock on which I might bend my knees. I seemed literally to be running a race with some confusion to which he was about to reduce me, but I felt that he had got in first when, before we had even entered the churchyard, he threw out—

"I want my own sort!"

It literally made me bound forward. "There are not many of your own sort, Miles!" I laughed. "Unless perhaps dear little Flora!"

"You really compare me to a baby girl?"

This found me singularly weak. "Don't you, then, LOVE our sweet Flora?"

"If I didn't—and you, too; if I didn't—!" he repeated as if retreating for a jump, yet leaving his thought so unfinished that, after we had come into the gate, another stop, which he imposed on me by the pressure of his arm, had become inevitable. Mrs. Grose and Flora had passed into the church, the other worshippers had followed, and we were, for the minute, alone among the old, thick graves. We had paused, on the path from the gate, by a low, oblong, tablelike tomb.

"Yes, if you didn't—?"

He looked, while I waited, at the graves. "Well, you know what!" But he didn't move, and he presently produced something that made me drop straight down on the stone slab, as if suddenly to rest. "Does my uncle think what YOU think?"

I markedly rested. "How do you know what I think?"

"Ah, well, of course I don't; for it strikes me you never tell me. But I mean does HE know?"

"Know what, Miles?"

"Why, the way I'm going on."

I perceived quickly enough that I could make, to this inquiry, no answer that would not involve something of a sacrifice of my employer. Yet it appeared to me that we were all, at Bly, sufficiently sacrificed to make that venial. "I don't think your uncle much cares."

Miles, on this, stood looking at me. "Then don't you think he can be made to?"

"In what way?"

"Why, by his coming down."

"But who'll get him to come down?"

"I will!" the boy said with extraordinary brightness and emphasis. He gave me another look charged with that expression and then marched off alone into church.

## Questions

What does Miles ask the governess as they are going to church?

Why does Miles want to go back to school?

What is the governess's response?

What does the governess tell Miles about their uncle?

What does Miles say he will make his uncle do?

GCSE style question: how does James make Miles such an interesting and defiant character in this chapter?

A Level style question: compare and contrast the representation of Miles with another representation of a similar character in a relevant text of your choice.

. Creative response: write Miles's diary for this chapter.

You can find brief answers in the section, **Answers to the Questions**.

# Chapter 15

The business was practically settled from the moment I never followed him. It was a pitiful surrender to agitation, but my being aware of this had somehow no power to restore me. I only sat there on my tomb and read into what my little friend had said to me the fullness of its meaning; by the time I had grasped the whole of which I had also embraced, for absence, the pretext that I was ashamed to offer my pupils and the rest of the congregation such an example of delay. What I said to myself above all was that Miles had got something out of me and that the proof of it, for him, would be just this awkward collapse. He had got out of me that there was something I was much afraid of and that he should probably be able to make use of my fear to gain, for his own purpose, more freedom. My fear was of having to deal with the intolerable question of the grounds of his dismissal from school, for that was really but the question of the horrors gathered behind. That his uncle should arrive to treat with me of these things was a solution that, strictly speaking, I ought now to have desired to bring on; but I could so little face the ugliness and the pain of it that I simply procrastinated and lived from hand to mouth. The boy, to my deep discomposure, was immensely in the right, was in a position to say to me: "Either you clear up with my guardian the mystery of this interruption of my studies, or you cease to expect me to lead with you a life that's so unnatural for a boy." What was so unnatural for the particular boy I was concerned with was this sudden revelation of a consciousness and a plan.

That was what really overcame me, what prevented my going in. I walked round the church, hesitating, hovering; I reflected that I had already, with him, hurt myself beyond repair. Therefore I could patch up nothing, and it was too extreme an effort to squeeze beside him into the pew: he would be so much more sure than ever to pass his arm into mine and make me sit there for an hour in close, silent contact with his commentary on our talk. For the first minute since his arrival I wanted to get away from him. As I paused beneath the high east window and listened to the sounds of worship, I was taken with an impulse that might master me, I felt, completely should I give it the least encouragement. I might easily put an end to my predicament by getting away altogether. Here was my chance; there was no one to stop me; I could give the whole thing up—turn my back and retreat. It was only a question of hurrying again, for a few preparations, to the house which the attendance at church of so many of the servants would practically have left unoccupied. No one, in short, could blame me if I should just drive desperately off. What was it to get away if I got away only till dinner? That would be in a couple of hours, at the end of which—I had the acute prevision—my little pupils would play at innocent wonder about my nonappearance in their train.

"What DID you do, you naughty, bad thing? Why in the world, to worry us so—and take our thoughts off, too, don't you know?—did you desert us at the very door?" I couldn't meet such questions nor, as they asked them, their false little lovely eyes; yet it was all so exactly what I should have to meet that, as the prospect grew sharp to me, I at last let myself go.

I got, so far as the immediate moment was concerned, away; I came straight out of the churchyard and, thinking hard, retraced my steps through the park. It seemed to me that by the time I reached the house I had made up my mind I would fly. The Sunday stillness both of the approaches and of the interior, in which I met no one, fairly excited me with a sense of opportunity. Were I to get off quickly, this way, I should get off without a scene, without a word. My quickness would have to be remarkable, however, and the question of a conveyance was the great one to settle. Tormented, in the hall, with difficulties and obstacles, I remember sinking down at the foot of the staircase—suddenly collapsing there on the lowest step and then, with a revulsion, recalling that it was exactly where more than a month before, in the darkness of night and just so bowed with evil things, I had seen the specter of the most horrible of women. At this I was able to straighten myself; I went the rest of the way up; I made, in my bewilderment, for the schoolroom, where there were objects belonging to me that I should have to take. But I opened the door to find again, in a flash, my eyes unsealed. In the presence of what I saw I reeled straight back upon my resistance.

Seated at my own table in clear noonday light I saw a person whom, without my previous experience, I should have taken at the first blush for some housemaid who might have stayed at home to look after the place and who, availing herself of rare relief from observation and of the schoolroom table and my pens, ink, and paper, had applied herself to the considerable effort of a letter to her sweetheart. There was an effort in the way that, while her arms rested on the table, her hands with evident weariness supported her head; but at the moment I took this in I had already become aware that, in spite of my entrance, her attitude strangely persisted. Then it was—with the very act of its announcing itself—that her identity flared up in a change of posture. She rose, not as if she had heard me, but with an indescribable grand melancholy of indifference and detachment, and, within a dozen feet of me, stood there as my vile predecessor. Dishonored and tragic, she was all before me; but even as I fixed and, for memory, secured it, the awful image passed away. Dark as midnight in her black dress, her haggard beauty and her unutterable woe, she had looked at me long enough to appear to say that her right to sit at my table was as good as mine to sit at hers. While these instants lasted, indeed, I had the extraordinary chill of feeling that it was I who was the intruder. It was as a wild protest against it that, actually addressing her—"You terrible, miserable woman!"—I heard myself break into a sound that, by the open door, rang through the long passage and the empty house. She looked at me as if she heard me, but I had recovered myself and cleared the air. There was nothing in the room the next minute but the sunshine and a sense that I must stay.

Analysis: The governess's next sighting of Miss Jessel is all the more haunting because she appears to be a sort of 'reverse' mirror image of the governess herself. The governess has sort, above all, to be honourable and triumphant, to keep away the ghosts, to bring up the children properly, to do the right thing. Miss Jessel is the opposite to this: she is 'dishonoured and tragic'. She has been brought down low by her sexual relationship with Quint, by her ghostliness, and is tragically unhappy as a consequence. But this is, in a sense, a mirror of image of what the governess could be: she is obviously attracted to the master of the house, has sexual desires of her own, and could easily be drawn into her own tragedy and disgrace. She shouts at her so strongly because Miss Jessel sits at her table, which, interpreted metaphorically, could mean that Miss Jessel is very similar to her. Of course, this is something that the governess realises about herself: she sees herself as a good person combating the evil of the ghosts. Her shouting at the ghost: "You terrible, miserable woman!" shows her determination to take on the ghosts on one level. It could be another indication that she is gradually losing her mind. The sighting prompts her to stay and to later write to her employer as Mrs Grose advised previously.

Discussion point: Why is this a particularly haunting point in the novel?

## Questions

What shocks the governess about Miles?

What does the governess decide to do?

Why does the governess change her mind?

GCSE style question: how does James make the sighting of Miss Jessel such a suspenseful and terrifying moment?

Creative response: write Miss Jessel's diary entry for this chapter and previous relevant chapters.

Creative response: write a description of what you think happened between Miss Jessel, Peter Quint and the children.

You can find brief answers in the section, **Answers to the Questions**.

# Chapter 16

I had so perfectly expected that the return of my pupils would be marked by a demonstration that I was freshly upset at having to take into account that they were dumb about my absence. Instead of gaily denouncing and caressing me, they made no allusion to my having failed them, and I was left, for the time, on perceiving that she too said nothing, to study Mrs. Grose's odd face. I did this to such purpose that I made sure they had in some way bribed her to silence; a silence that, however, I would engage to break down on the first private opportunity. This opportunity came before tea: I secured five minutes with her in the housekeeper's room, where, in the twilight, amid a smell of lately baked bread, but with the place all swept and garnished, I found her sitting in pained placidity before the fire. So I see her still, so I see her best: facing the flame from her straight chair in the dusky, shining room, a large clean image of the "put away"—of drawers closed and locked and rest without a remedy.

"Oh, yes, they asked me to say nothing; and to please them—so long as they were there—of course I promised. But what had happened to you?"

"I only went with you for the walk," I said. "I had then to come back to meet a friend."

She showed her surprise. "A friend—YOU?"

"Oh, yes, I have a couple!" I laughed. "But did the children give you a reason?"

"For not alluding to your leaving us? Yes; they said you would like it better. Do you like it better?"

My face had made her rueful. "No, I like it worse!" But after an instant I added: "Did they say why I should like it better?"

"No; Master Miles only said, 'We must do nothing but what she likes!'"

"I wish indeed he would. And what did Flora say?"

"Miss Flora was too sweet. She said, 'Oh, of course, of course!'—and I said the same."

I thought a moment. "You were too sweet, too—I can hear you all. But nonetheless, between Miles and me, it's now all out."

"All out?" My companion stared. "But what, miss?"

"Everything. It doesn't matter. I've made up my mind. I came home, my dear," I went on, "for a talk with Miss Jessel."

I had by this time formed the habit of having Mrs. Grose literally well in hand in advance of my sounding that note; so that even now, as she bravely blinked under the signal of my word, I could keep her comparatively firm. "A talk! Do you mean she spoke?"

"It came to that. I found her, on my return, in the schoolroom."

"And what did she say?" I can hear the good woman still, and the candor of her stupefaction.

"That she suffers the torments—!"

It was this, of a truth, that made her, as she filled out my picture, gape. "Do you mean," she faltered, "—of the lost?"

"Of the lost. Of the damned. And that's why, to share them-" I faltered myself with the horror of it.

But my companion, with less imagination, kept me up. "To share them—?"

"She wants Flora." Mrs. Grose might, as I gave it to her, fairly have fallen away from me had I not been prepared. I still held her there, to show I was. "As I've told you, however, it doesn't matter."

"Because you've made up your mind? But to what?"

"To everything."

"And what do you call 'everything'?"

"Why, sending for their uncle."

"Oh, miss, in pity do," my friend broke out. "ah, but I will, I WILL! I see it's the only way. What's 'out,' as I told you, with Miles is that if he thinks I'm afraid to—and has ideas of what he gains by that—he shall see he's mistaken. Yes, yes; his uncle shall have it here from me on the spot (and before the boy himself, if necessary) that if I'm to be reproached with having done nothing again about more school—"

"Yes, miss—" my companion pressed me.

"Well, there's that awful reason."

There were now clearly so many of these for my poor colleague that she was excusable for being vague. "But—a—which?"

"Why, the letter from his old place."

"You'll show it to the master?"

"I ought to have done so on the instant."

"Oh, no!" said Mrs. Grose with decision.

"I'll put it before him," I went on inexorably, "that I can't undertake to work the question on behalf of a child who has been expelled—"

"For we've never in the least known what!" Mrs. Grose declared.

"For wickedness. For what else—when he's so clever and beautiful and perfect? Is he stupid? Is he untidy? Is he infirm? Is he ill-natured? He's exquisite—so it can be only THAT; and that would open up the whole thing. After all," I said, "it's their uncle's fault. If he left here such people—!"

"He didn't really in the least know them. The fault's mine." She had turned quite pale.

"Well, you shan't suffer," I answered.

"The children shan't!" she emphatically returned.

I was silent awhile; we looked at each other. "Then what am I to tell him?"

"You needn't tell him anything. I'll tell him."

I measured this. "Do you mean you'll write—?" Remembering she couldn't, I caught myself up. "How do you communicate?"

"I tell the bailiff. HE writes."

"And should you like him to write our story?"

My question had a sarcastic force that I had not fully intended, and it made her, after a moment, inconsequently break down. The tears were again in her eyes. "Ah, miss, YOU write!"

"Well—tonight," I at last answered; and on this we separated.

## Questions

What does Mrs Grose tell the governess the children have said when they get back from church?

What does the governess say happened with her and Miss Jessel?

What does the governess say which pleases Mrs Grose?

What does the governess now think was the reason for Miles's expulsion from school?

Why is the governess reluctant to write to the uncle?

What is finally agreed and why?

GCSE style question: how and why is the governess proved to be an unreliable narrator in this chapter?

GCSE style question: how does James develop the character of Mrs Grose in this chapter?

A Level style question: compare and contrast unreliable narrators in this text and another relevant one of your choice.

Creative response: write Mrs Grose's diary for this chapter.

Creative response: write a first person description of an incident such as an account of bullying/sighting of a ghost, but make sure you reveal in the telling that the narrator is possibly unreliable, deliberately putting inconsistencies into the account.

You can find brief answers in the section, **Answers to the Questions**.

# Chapter 17

I went so far, in the evening, as to make a beginning. The weather had changed back, a great wind was abroad, and beneath the lamp, in my room, with Flora at peace beside me, I sat for a long time before a blank sheet of paper and listened to the lash of the rain and the batter of the gusts. Finally I went out, taking a candle; I crossed the passage and listened a minute at Miles's door. What, under my endless obsession, I had been impelled to listen for was some betrayal of his not being at rest, and I presently caught one, but not in the form I had expected. His voice tinkled out. "I say, you there—come in." It was a gaiety in the gloom!

I went in with my light and found him, in bed, very wide awake, but very much at his ease. "Well, what are YOU up to?" he asked with a grace of sociability in which it occurred to me that Mrs. Grose, had she been present, might have looked in vain for proof that anything was "out."

I stood over him with my candle. "How did you know I was there?"

"Why, of course I heard you. Did you fancy you made no noise? You're like a troop of cavalry!" he beautifully laughed.

"Then you weren't asleep?"

"Not much! I lie awake and think."

I had put my candle, designedly, a short way off, and then, as he held out his friendly old hand to me, had sat down on the edge of his bed. "What is it," I asked, "that you think of?"

"What in the world, my dear, but YOU?"

"Ah, the pride I take in your appreciation doesn't insist on that! I had so far rather you slept."

"Well, I think also, you know, of this queer business of ours."

I marked the coolness of his firm little hand. "Of what queer business, Miles?"

"Why, the way you bring me up. And all the rest!"

I fairly held my breath a minute, and even from my glimmering taper there was light enough to show how he smiled up at me from his pillow. "What do you mean by all the rest?"

"Oh, you know, you know!"

I could say nothing for a minute, though I felt, as I held his hand and our eyes continued to meet, that my silence had all the air of admitting his charge and that nothing in the whole world of reality was perhaps at that moment so fabulous as our actual relation. "Certainly you shall go back to school," I said, "if it be that that troubles you. But not to the old place—we must find another, a better. How could I know it did trouble you, this question, when you never told me so, never spoke of it at all?" His clear, listening face, framed in its smooth whiteness, made him for the minute as appealing as some wistful patient in a children's hospital; and I would have given, as the resemblance came to me, all I possessed on earth really to be the nurse or the sister of charity who might have helped to cure him. Well, even as it was, I perhaps might help! "Do you know you've never said a word to me about your school—I mean the old one; never mentioned it in any way?"

He seemed to wonder; he smiled with the same loveliness. But he clearly gained time; he waited, he called for guidance. "Haven't I?" It wasn't for ME to help him—it was for the thing I had met!

Something in his tone and the expression of his face, as I got this from him, set my heart aching with such a pang as it had never yet known; so unutterably touching was it to see his little brain puzzled and his little resources taxed to play, under the spell laid on him, a part of innocence and consistency. "No, never—from the hour you came back. You've never mentioned to me one of your masters, one of your comrades, nor the least little thing that ever happened to you at school. Never, little Miles—no, never—have you given me an inkling of anything that MAY have happened there. Therefore you can fancy how much I'm in the dark. Until you came out, that way, this morning, you had, since the first hour I saw you, scarce even made a reference to anything in your previous life. You seemed so perfectly to accept the present." It was extraordinary how my absolute conviction of his secret precocity (or whatever I might call the poison of an influence that I dared but half to phrase) made him, in spite of the faint breath of his inward trouble, appear as accessible as an older person— imposed him almost as an intellectual equal. "I thought you wanted to go on as you are."

It struck me that at this he just faintly colored. He gave, at any rate, like a convalescent slightly fatigued, a languid shake of his head. "I don't—I don't. I want to get away."

"You're tired of Bly?"

"Oh, no, I like Bly."

"Well, then—?"

"Oh, YOU know what a boy wants!"

I felt that I didn't know so well as Miles, and I took temporary refuge. "You want to go to your uncle?"

Again, at this, with his sweet ironic face, he made a movement on the pillow. "Ah, you can't get off with that!"

I was silent a little, and it was I, now, I think, who changed color. "My dear, I don't want to get off!"

"You can't, even if you do. You can't, you can't!"—he lay beautifully staring. "My uncle must come down, and you must completely settle things."

"If we do," I returned with some spirit, "you may be sure it will be to take you quite away."

"Well, don't you understand that that's exactly what I'm working for? You'll have to tell him—about the way you've let it all drop: you'll have to tell him a tremendous lot!"

The exultation with which he uttered this helped me somehow, for the instant, to meet him rather more. "And how much will YOU, Miles, have to tell him? There are things he'll ask you!"

He turned it over. "Very likely. But what things?"

"The things you've never told me. To make up his mind what to do with you. He can't send you back—"

"Oh, I don't want to go back!" he broke in. "I want a new field."

He said it with admirable serenity, with positive unimpeachable gaiety; and doubtless it was that very note that most evoked for me the poignancy, the unnatural childish tragedy, of his probable reappearance at the end of three months with all this bravado and still more dishonor. It overwhelmed me now that I should never be able to bear that, and it made me let myself go. I threw myself upon him and in the tenderness of my pity I embraced him. "Dear little Miles, dear little Miles—!"

My face was close to his, and he let me kiss him, simply taking it with indulgent good humor. "Well, old lady?"

"Is there nothing—nothing at all that you want to tell me?"

He turned off a little, facing round toward the wall and holding up his hand to look at as one had seen sick children look. "I've told you—I told you this morning."

Oh, I was sorry for him! "That you just want me not to worry you?"

He looked round at me now, as if in recognition of my understanding him; then ever so gently, "To let me alone," he replied.

There was even a singular little dignity in it, something that made me release him, yet, when I had slowly risen, linger beside him. God knows I never wished to harass him, but I felt that merely, at this, to turn my back on him was to abandon or, to put it more truly, to lose him. "I've just begun a letter to your uncle," I said.

"Well, then, finish it!"

I waited a minute. "What happened before?"

He gazed up at me again. "Before what?"

"Before you came back. And before you went away."

For some time he was silent, but he continued to meet my eyes. "What happened?"

It made me, the sound of the words, in which it seemed to me that I caught for the very first time a small faint quaver of consenting consciousness—it made me drop on my knees beside the bed and seize once more the chance of possessing him. "Dear little Miles, dear little Miles, if you KNEW how I want to help you! It's only that, it's nothing but that, and I'd rather die than give you a pain or do you a wrong—I'd rather die than hurt a hair of you. Dear little Miles"—oh, I brought it out now even if I SHOULD go too far—"I just want you to help me to save you!" But I knew in a moment after this that I had gone too far. The answer to my appeal was instantaneous, but it came in the form of an extraordinary blast and chill, a gust of frozen air, and a shake of the room as great as if, in the wild wind, the casement had crashed in. The boy gave a loud, high shriek, which, lost in the rest of the shock of sound, might have seemed, indistinctly, though I was so close to him, a note either of jubilation or of terror. I jumped to my feet again and was conscious of darkness. So for a moment we remained, while I stared about me and saw that the drawn curtains were unstirred and the window tight. "Why, the candle's out!" I then cried.

"It was I who blew it, dear!" said Miles.

Analysis: Here we see the governess feeling that the situation is increasingly desperate. She drops on her knees by his bed – like she is praying or begging before him – and states her case: "I just want you to help me to save you." The phrasing is interesting here because she doesn't say that she wants to help him directly. She wants him to open up to her, to take her into her confidence about the ghosts. In other words, she needs the children to endorse the narrative about the ghosts. The "gust of frozen air" is a wonderfully dramatic and ambiguous moment. Is it a ghost or is it merely a gust of air? The governess' description of Miles' shriek is fascinating: it has either "jubilation or terror" about it.

**Discussion point:** Is Miles jubilant or terrified? Does he blow the candle out or is he covering for the ghosts? How is James increasing the sense of horror and claustrophobia here?

## Questions

Why does the governess stop writing the letter?

What is Miles bothered about? What reason does the governess give for not sending Miles back to school?

Why does the governess embrace and kiss Miles?

Why does Miles shriek?

GCSE style question: how does James make the relationship between Miles and the governess such an intense and fascinating one?

A Level style questions: compare and contrast the intense adult/child relationships in this story with another relevant text of your choice.

Creative response: write Miles's diary for this chapter.

You can find brief answers in the section, **Answers to the Questions**.

# Chapter 18

The next day, after lessons, Mrs. Grose found a moment to say to me quietly: "Have you written, miss?"

"Yes—I've written." But I didn't add—for the hour—that my letter, sealed and directed, was still in my pocket. There would be time enough to send it before the messenger should go to the village. Meanwhile there had been, on the part of my pupils, no more brilliant, more exemplary morning. It was exactly as if they had both had at heart to gloss over any recent little friction. They performed the dizziest feats of arithmetic, soaring quite out of MY feeble range, and perpetrated, in higher spirits than ever, geographical and historical jokes. It was conspicuous of course in Miles in particular that he appeared to wish to show how easily he could let me down. This child, to my memory, really lives in a setting of beauty and misery that no words can translate; there was a distinction all his own in every impulse he revealed; never was a small natural creature, to the uninitiated eye all frankness and freedom, a more ingenious, a more extraordinary little gentleman. I had perpetually to guard against the wonder of contemplation into which my initiated view betrayed me; to check the irrelevant gaze and discouraged sigh in which I constantly both attacked and renounced the enigma of what such a little gentleman could have done that deserved a penalty. Say that, by the dark prodigy I knew, the imagination of all evil HAD been opened up to him: all the justice within me ached for the proof that it could ever have flowered into an act.

He had never, at any rate, been such a little gentleman as when, after our early dinner on this dreadful day, he came round to me and asked if I shouldn't like him, for half an hour, to play to me. David playing to Saul could never have shown a finer sense of the occasion. It was literally a charming exhibition of tact, of magnanimity, and quite tantamount to his saying outright: "The true knights we love to read about never push an advantage too far. I know what you mean now: you mean that—to be let alone yourself and not followed up—you'll cease to worry and spy upon me, won't keep me so close to you, will let me go and come. Well, I 'come,' you see—but I don't go! There'll be plenty of time for that. I do really delight in your society, and I only want to show you that I contended for a principle." It may be imagined whether I resisted this appeal or failed to accompany him again, hand in hand, to the schoolroom. He sat down at the old piano and played as he had never played; and if there are those who think he had better have been kicking a football I can only say that I wholly agree with them. For at the end of a time that under his influence I had quite ceased to measure, I started up with a strange sense of having literally slept at my post. It was after luncheon, and by the schoolroom fire, and yet I hadn't really, in the least, slept: I had only done something much worse—I had forgotten. Where, all this time, was Flora? When I put the question to Miles, he played on a minute before answering and then could only say: "Why, my dear, how do I know?"—breaking moreover into a happy laugh which, immediately after, as if it were a vocal accompaniment, he prolonged into incoherent, extravagant song.

I went straight to my room, but his sister was not there; then, before going downstairs, I looked into several others. As she was nowhere about she would surely be with Mrs. Grose, whom, in the comfort of that theory, I accordingly proceeded in quest of. I found her where I had found her the evening before, but she met my quick challenge with blank, scared ignorance. She had only supposed that, after the repast, I had carried off both the children; as to which she was quite in her right, for it was the very first time I had allowed the little girl out of my sight without some special provision. Of course now indeed she might be with the maids, so that the immediate thing was to look for her without an air of alarm. This we promptly arranged between us; but when, ten minutes later and in pursuance of our arrangement, we met in the hall, it was only to report on either side that after guarded inquiries we had altogether failed to trace her. For a minute there, apart from observation, we exchanged mute alarms, and I could feel with what high interest my friend returned me all those I had from the first given her.

"She'll be above," she presently said—"in one of the rooms you haven't searched."

"No; she's at a distance." I had made up my mind. "She has gone out."

Mrs. Grose stared. "Without a hat?"

I naturally also looked volumes. "Isn't that woman always without one?"

"She's with HER?"

"She's with HER!" I declared. "We must find them."

My hand was on my friend's arm, but she failed for the moment, confronted with such an account of the matter, to respond to my pressure.

She communed, on the contrary, on the spot, with her uneasiness. "And where's Master Miles?"

"Oh, HE'S with Quint. They're in the schoolroom."

"Lord, miss!" My view, I was myself aware—and therefore I suppose my tone—had never yet reached so calm an assurance.

"The trick's played," I went on; "they've successfully worked their plan. He found the most divine little way to keep me quiet while she went off."

"'Divine'?" Mrs. Grose bewilderedly echoed.

"Infernal, then!" I almost cheerfully rejoined. "He has provided for himself as well. But come!"

She had helplessly gloomed at the upper regions. "You leave him—?"

"So long with Quint? Yes—I don't mind that now."

She always ended, at these moments, by getting possession of my hand, and in this manner she could at present still stay me. But after gasping an instant at my sudden resignation, "Because of your letter?" she eagerly brought out.

I quickly, by way of answer, felt for my letter, drew it forth, held it up, and then, freeing myself, went and laid it on the great hall table. "Luke will take it," I said as I came back. I reached the house door and opened it; I was already on the steps.

Analysis: Now the governess' desperation to catch the children with the ghosts, to prove everything to Mrs Grose becomes paramount. The dialogue is very tense, and the governess is increasingly unbalanced. She had to leave Miles alone while she wrote to her employer.

Discussion point: How does James build the tension here?

My companion still demurred: the storm of the night and the early morning had dropped, but the afternoon was damp and gray. I came down to the drive while she stood in the doorway. "You go with nothing on?"

"What do I care when the child has nothing? I can't wait to dress," I cried, "and if you must do so, I leave you. Try meanwhile, yourself, upstairs."

"With THEM?" Oh, on this, the poor woman promptly joined me!

## Questions

What does Mrs Grose ask the governess about and why is her answer not the whole truth?

What does Miles ask for which pleases the governess?

What does the governess realise as she is playing the piano?

What does the governess think Miles is doing?

GCSE style question: how does James present the battle of wills between Miles and the governess in this chapter?

A Level style question: compare and contrast the battle of wills in this story with another one in a relevant text.

Creative response: write Miles's diary for this chapter.

You can find brief answers in the section, **Answers to the Questions**.

# Chapter 19

We went straight to the lake, as it was called at Bly, and I daresay rightly called, though I reflect that it may in fact have been a sheet of water less remarkable than it appeared to my untraveled eyes. My acquaintance with sheets of water was small, and the pool of Bly, at all events on the few occasions of my consenting, under the protection of my pupils, to affront its surface in the old flat-bottomed boat moored there for our use, had impressed me both with its extent and its agitation. The usual place of embarkation was half a mile from the house, but I had an intimate conviction that, wherever Flora might be, she was not near home. She had not given me the slip for any small adventure, and, since the day of the very great one that I had shared with her by the pond, I had been aware, in our walks, of the quarter to which she most inclined. This was why I had now given to Mrs. Grose's steps so marked a direction—a direction that made her, when she perceived it, oppose a resistance that showed me she was freshly mystified. "You're going to the water, Miss?—you think she's IN—?"

"She may be, though the depth is, I believe, nowhere very great. But what I judge most likely is that she's on the spot from which, the other day, we saw together what I told you."

"When she pretended not to see—?"

"With that astounding self-possession? I've always been sure she wanted to go back alone. And now her brother has managed it for her."

Mrs. Grose still stood where she had stopped. "You suppose they really TALK of them?"

"I could meet this with a confidence! They say things that, if we heard them, would simply appall us."

"And if she IS there—"

"Yes?"

"Then Miss Jessel is?"

"Beyond a doubt. You shall see."

"Oh, thank you!" my friend cried, planted so firm that, taking it in, I went straight on without her. By the time I reached the pool, however, she was close behind me, and I knew that, whatever, to her apprehension, might befall me, the exposure of my society struck her as her least danger. She exhaled a moan of relief as we at last came in sight of the greater part of the water without a sight of the child. There was no trace of Flora on that nearer side of the bank where my observation of her had been most startling, and none on the opposite edge, where, save for a margin of some twenty yards, a thick copse came down to the water. The pond, oblong in shape, had a width so scant compared to its length that, with its ends out of view, it might have been taken for a scant river. We looked at the empty expanse, and then I felt the suggestion of my friend's eyes. I knew what she meant and I replied with a negative headshake.

"No, no; wait! She has taken the boat."

My companion stared at the vacant mooring place and then again across the lake. "Then where is it?"

"Our not seeing it is the strongest of proofs. She has used it to go over, and then has managed to hide it."

"All alone—that child?"

"She's not alone, and at such times she's not a child: she's an old, old woman." I scanned all the visible shore while Mrs. Grose took again, into the queer element I offered her, one of her plunges of submission; then I pointed out that the boat might perfectly be in a small refuge formed by one of the recesses of the pool, an indentation masked, for the hither side, by a projection of the bank and by a clump of trees growing close to the water.

"But if the boat's there, where on earth's SHE?" my colleague anxiously asked.

"That's exactly what we must learn." And I started to walk further.

"By going all the way round?"

"Certainly, far as it is. It will take us but ten minutes, but it's far enough to have made the child prefer not to walk. She went straight over."

"Laws!" cried my friend again; the chain of my logic was ever too much for her. It dragged her at my heels even now, and when we had got halfway round—a devious, tiresome process, on ground much broken and by a path choked with overgrowth—I paused to give her breath. I sustained her with a grateful arm, assuring her that she might hugely help me; and this started us afresh, so that in the course of but few minutes more we reached a point from which we found the boat to be where I had supposed it. It had been intentionally left as much as possible out of sight and was tied to one of the stakes of a fence that came, just there, down to the brink and that had been an assistance to disembarking. I recognized, as I looked at the pair of short, thick oars, quite safely drawn up, the prodigious character of the feat for a little girl; but I had lived, by this time, too long among wonders and had panted to too many livelier measures. There was a gate in the fence, through which we passed, and that brought us, after a trifling interval, more into the open. Then, "There she is!" we both exclaimed at once.

Flora, a short way off, stood before us on the grass and smiled as if her performance was now complete. The next thing she did, however, was to stoop straight down and pluck—quite as if it were all she was there for—a big, ugly spray of withered fern. I instantly became sure she had just come out of the copse. She waited for us, not herself taking a step, and I was conscious of the rare solemnity with which we presently approached her. She smiled and smiled, and we met; but it was all done in a silence by this time flagrantly ominous. Mrs. Grose was the first to break the spell: she threw herself on her knees and, drawing the child to her breast, clasped in a long embrace the little tender, yielding body. While this dumb convulsion lasted I could only watch it—which I did the more intently when I saw Flora's face peep at me over our companion's shoulder. It was serious now—the flicker had left it; but it strengthened the pang with which I at that moment envied Mrs. Grose the simplicity of HER relation. Still, all this while, nothing more passed between us save that Flora had let her foolish fern again drop to the ground. What she and I had virtually said to each other was that pretexts were useless now. When Mrs. Grose finally got up she kept the child's hand, so that the two were still before me; and the singular reticence of our communion was even more marked in the frank look she launched me. "I'll be hanged," it said, "if I'll speak!"

It was Flora who, gazing all over me in candid wonder, was the first. She was struck with our bareheaded aspect. "Why, where are your things?"

"Where yours are, my dear!" I promptly returned.

She had already got back her gaiety, and appeared to take this as an answer quite sufficient. "And where's Miles?" she went on.

There was something in the small valor of it that quite finished me: these three words from her were, in a flash like the glitter of a drawn blade, the jostle of the cup that my hand, for weeks and weeks, had held high and full to the brim that now, even before speaking, I felt overflow in a deluge. "I'll tell you if you'll tell ME—" I heard myself say, then heard the tremor in which it broke.

"Well, what?"

Mrs. Grose's suspense blazed at me, but it was too late now, and I brought the thing out handsomely. "Where, my pet, is Miss Jessel?"

Analysis: The moment of real confrontation has come. She asks the momentous question about whether Flora knows where Miss Jessel is. Notice how James describes Mrs Grose as holding Flora's hand – indicating that it is Mrs Grose who is the real guardian for the children.

Discussion point: How could Flora's look at the governess be interpreted? Is it defiant or dumbfounded because the little girl does not know what is going on?

## Questions

Where do the governess and Mrs Grose head to and why?

Where do they find Flora?

What does Flora appear to be puzzled about?

What does governess say Flora must do?

GCSE style question: how does James generate suspense with Flora's disappearance in this chapter?

A Level style question: compare and contrast the disappearance of Flora in this chapter with another disappearance in a relevant text.

Creative response: write Flora's diary for this chapter.

Creative response: predict what might happen next.

You can find brief answers in the section, **Answers to the Questions**.

# Chapter 20

Just as in the churchyard with Miles, the whole thing was upon us. Much as I had made of the fact that this name had never once, between us, been sounded, the quick, smitten glare with which the child's face now received it fairly likened my breach of the silence to the smash of a pane of glass. It added to the interposing cry, as if to stay the blow, that Mrs. Grose, at the same instant, uttered over my violence—the shriek of a creature scared, or rather wounded, which, in turn, within a few seconds, was completed by a gasp of my own. I seized my colleague's arm. "She's there, she's there!"

Miss Jessel stood before us on the opposite bank exactly as she had stood the other time, and I remember, strangely, as the first feeling now produced in me, my thrill of joy at having brought on a proof. She was there, and I was justified; she was there, and I was neither cruel nor mad. She was there for poor scared Mrs. Grose, but she was there most for Flora; and no moment of my monstrous time was perhaps so extraordinary as that in which I consciously threw out to her—with the sense that, pale and ravenous demon as she was, she would catch and understand it—an inarticulate message of gratitude. She rose erect on the spot my friend and I had lately quitted, and there was not, in all the long reach of her desire, an inch of her evil that fell short. This first vividness of vision and emotion were things of a few seconds, during which Mrs. Grose's dazed blink across to where I pointed struck me as a sovereign sign that she too at last saw, just as it carried my own eyes precipitately to the child. The revelation then of the manner in which Flora was affected startled me, in truth, far more than it would have done to find her also merely agitated, for direct dismay was of course not what I had expected. Prepared and on her guard as our pursuit had actually made her, she would repress every betrayal; and I was therefore shaken, on the spot, by my first glimpse of the particular one for which I had not allowed. To see her, without a convulsion of her small pink face, not even feign to glance in the direction of the prodigy I announced, but only, instead of that, turn at ME an expression of hard, still gravity, an expression absolutely new and unprecedented and that appeared to read and accuse and judge me—this was a stroke that somehow converted the little girl herself into the very presence that could make me quail. I quailed even though my certitude that she thoroughly saw was never greater than at that instant, and in the immediate need to defend myself I called it passionately to witness. "She's there, you little unhappy thing—there, there, THERE, and you see her as well as you see me!" I had said shortly before to Mrs. Grose that she was not at these times a child, but an old, old woman, and that description of her could not have been more strikingly confirmed than in the way in which, for all answer to this, she simply showed me, without a concession, an admission, of her eyes, a countenance of deeper and deeper, of indeed suddenly quite fixed, reprobation. I was by this time—if I can put the whole thing at all together—more appalled at what I may properly call her manner than at anything else, though it was simultaneously with this that I became aware of having Mrs. Grose also, and very formidably, to reckon with. My elder companion, the next moment, at any rate, blotted out everything but her own flushed face and her loud, shocked protest, a burst of high disapproval. "What a dreadful turn, to be sure, miss! Where on earth do you see anything?"

Analysis: This is a vital moment. Mrs Grose does not believe that there are any ghosts. The description of the housekeeper is important here: she has a "flushed face", and speaks with a "burst of high disapproval". Finally, we see that Mrs Grose has no belief in the governess. Her words are very telling: "What a dreadful turn, to be sure, miss! Where on earth do you see anything?" The metaphor of the word "turn" is important: this is the "turn of the screw", the moment of revelation, the moment when the truth is revealed. Except that it isn't!

Discussion point: What do you think of the presentation of Mrs Grose here? What does it reveal about her?

I could only grasp her more quickly yet, for even while she spoke the hideous plain presence stood undimmed and undaunted. It had already lasted a minute, and it lasted while I continued, seizing my colleague, quite thrusting her at it and presenting her to it, to insist with my pointing hand. "You don't see her exactly as WE see?—you mean to say you don't now—NOW? She's as big as a blazing fire! Only look, dearest woman, LOOK—!" She looked, even as I did, and gave me, with her deep groan of negation, repulsion, compassion—the mixture with her pity of her relief at her exemption—a sense, touching to me even then, that she would have backed me up if she could. I might well have needed that, for with this hard blow of the proof that her eyes were hopelessly sealed I felt my own situation horribly crumble, I felt—I saw—my livid predecessor press, from her position, on my defeat, and I was conscious, more than all, of what I should have from this instant to deal with in the astounding little attitude of Flora. Into this attitude Mrs. Grose immediately and violently entered, breaking, even while there pierced through my sense of ruin a prodigious private triumph, into breathless reassurance.

"She isn't there, little lady, and nobody's there—and you never see nothing, my sweet! How can poor Miss Jessel—when poor Miss Jessel's dead and buried? WE know, don't we, love?"—and she appealed, blundering in, to the child. "It's all a mere mistake and a worry and a joke—and we'll go home as fast as we can!"

Our companion, on this, had responded with a strange, quick primness of propriety, and they were again, with Mrs. Grose on her feet, united, as it were, in pained opposition to me. Flora continued to fix me with her small mask of reprobation, and even at that minute I prayed God to forgive me for seeming to see that, as she stood there holding tight to our friend's dress, her incomparable childish beauty had suddenly failed, had quite vanished. I've said it already—she was literally, she was hideously, hard;

she had turned common and almost ugly. "I don't know what you mean. I see nobody. I see nothing. I never HAVE. I think you're cruel. I don't like you!" Then, after this deliverance, which might have been that of a vulgarly pert little girl in the street, she hugged Mrs. Grose more closely and buried in her skirts the dreadful little face. In this position she produced an almost furious wail. "Take me away, take me away—oh, take me away from HER!"

"From ME?" I panted.

"From you—from you!" she cried.

**Analysis:** Mrs Grose is either the voice of stupidity, of blindness, or of reason here. Victorian readers, believing her to be of a lower class, felt that she was the stupid one, not seeing what needed to be seen: the corrupting influence of the ghosts upon the young children. Modern readers, on the other hand, view Mrs Grose as the voice of reason, trying to establish some sanity, trying to make Flora feel more stable, amidst the madness. Flora then turns on the governess: she has a "mask of reprobation". Of course, the governess believes it to be a "mask" because she is hiding her real feelings of concern that the governess has found out the truth about her conspiracy with the ghosts. Notice how wonderfully accurately that James has caught the words and diction of a young child: "I think you're cruel. I don't like you!" If there are no ghosts, then these short, clear sentences perfectly convey the child's views: she's seen the governess' behaviour as a form of torture.

**Discussion point:** Mrs Grose sides with Flora here. What is the effect of this upon Flora, upon the governess, and upon the reader?

Even Mrs. Grose looked across at me dismayed, while I had nothing to do but communicate again with the figure that, on the opposite bank, without a movement, as rigidly still as if catching, beyond the interval, our voices, was as vividly there for my disaster as it was not there for my service. The wretched child had spoken exactly as if she had got from some outside source each of her stabbing little words, and I could therefore, in the full despair of all I had to accept, but sadly shake my head at her. "If I had ever doubted, all my doubt would at present have gone. I've been living with the miserable truth, and now it has only too much closed round me. Of course I've lost you: I've interfered, and you've seen—under HER dictation"—with which I faced, over the pool again, our infernal witness—"the easy and perfect way to meet it. I've done my best, but I've lost you. Goodbye." For Mrs. Grose I had an imperative, an almost frantic "Go, go!" before which, in infinite distress, but mutely possessed of the little girl and clearly convinced, in spite of her blindness, that something awful had occurred and some collapse engulfed us, she retreated, by the way we had come, as fast as she could move.

Of what first happened when I was left alone I had no subsequent memory. I only knew that at the end of, I suppose, a quarter of an hour, an odorous dampness and roughness, chilling and piercing my trouble, had made me understand that I must have thrown myself, on my face, on the ground and given way to a wildness of grief. I must have lain there long and cried and sobbed, for when I raised my head the day was almost done. I got up and looked a moment, through the twilight, at the gray pool and its blank, haunted edge, and then I took, back to the house, my dreary and difficult course. When I reached the gate in the fence the boat, to my surprise, was gone, so that I had a fresh reflection to make on Flora's extraordinary command of the situation. She passed that night, by the most tacit, and I should add, were not the word so grotesque a false note, the happiest of arrangements, with Mrs. Grose. I saw neither of them on my return, but, on the other hand, as by an ambiguous compensation, I saw a great deal of Miles. I saw—I can use no other phrase—so much of him that it was as if it were more than it had ever been. No evening I had passed at Bly had the portentous quality of this one; in spite of which—and in spite also of the deeper depths of consternation that had opened beneath my feet—there was literally, in the ebbing actual, an extraordinarily sweet sadness. On reaching the house I had never so much as looked for the boy; I had simply gone straight to my room to change what I was wearing and to take in, at a glance, much material testimony to Flora's rupture. Her little belongings had all been removed. When later, by the schoolroom fire, I was served with tea by the usual maid, I indulged, on the article of my other pupil, in no inquiry whatever. He had his freedom now—he might have it to the end! Well, he did have it; and it consisted—in part at least—of his coming in at about eight o'clock and sitting down with me in silence. On the removal of the tea things I had blown out the candles and drawn my chair closer: I was conscious of a mortal coldness and felt as if I should never again be warm. So, when he appeared, I was sitting in the glow with my thoughts. He paused a moment by the door as if to look at me; then—as if to share them—came to the other side of the hearth and sank into a chair. We sat there in absolute stillness; yet he wanted, I felt, to be with me.

## Questions

Where does the governess see Miss Jessel?

What does Mrs Grose see?

What does Flora insist Mrs Grose does?

What does the governess think has happened to Flora?

What does the governess notice about the position of the boat and why is this significant?

GCSE style question: how does James make Flora's plight both frightening and poignant in this chapter?

GCSE style question: how does James make the confrontation with Flora a climactic moment in the story?

A Level style question: compare and contrast the climax in this novel with another climatic moment in a relevant text of your choice.

Creative response: write Mrs Grose and Flora's diary entries for this chapter.

You can find brief answers in the section, **Answers to the Questions**.

# Chapter 21

Before a new day, in my room, had fully broken, my eyes opened to Mrs. Grose, who had come to my bedside with worse news. Flora was so markedly feverish that an illness was perhaps at hand; she had passed a night of extreme unrest, a night agitated above all by fears that had for their subject not in the least her former, but wholly her present, governess. It was not against the possible re-entrance of Miss Jessel on the scene that she protested—it was conspicuously and passionately against mine. I was promptly on my feet of course, and with an immense deal to ask; the more that my friend had discernibly now girded her loins to meet me once more. This I felt as soon as I had put to her the question of the child's sincerity as against my own. "She persists in denying to you that she saw, or has ever seen, anything?"

My visitor's trouble, truly, was great. "Ah, miss, it isn't a matter on which I can push her! Yet it isn't either, I must say, as if I much needed to. It has made her, every inch of her, quite old."

"Oh, I see her perfectly from here. She resents, for all the world like some high little personage, the imputation on her truthfulness and, as it were, her respectability. 'Miss Jessel indeed—SHE!' Ah, she's 'respectable,' the chit! The impression she gave me there yesterday was, I assure you, the very strangest of all; it was quite beyond any of the others. I DID put my foot in it! She'll never speak to me again."

Hideous and obscure as it all was, it held Mrs. Grose briefly silent; then she granted my point with a frankness which, I made sure, had more behind it. "I think indeed, miss, she never will. She do have a grand manner about it!"

"And that manner"—I summed it up—"is practically what's the matter with her now!"

Oh, that manner, I could see in my visitor's face, and not a little else besides! "She asks me every three minutes if I think you're coming in."

"I see—I see." I, too, on my side, had so much more than worked it out. "Has she said to you since yesterday—except to repudiate her familiarity with anything so dreadful—a single other word about Miss Jessel?"

"Not one, miss. And of course you know," my friend added, "I took it from her, by the lake, that, just then and there at least, there WAS nobody."

"Rather! and, naturally, you take it from her still."

"I don't contradict her. What else can I do?"

"Nothing in the world! You've the cleverest little person to deal with. They've made them—their two friends, I mean—still cleverer even than nature did; for it was wondrous material to play on! Flora has now her grievance, and she'll work it to the end."

"Yes, miss; but to WHAT end?"

"Why, that of dealing with me to her uncle. She'll make me out to him the lowest creature—!"

I winced at the fair show of the scene in Mrs. Grose's face; she looked for a minute as if she sharply saw them together. "And him who thinks so well of you!"

"He has an odd way—it comes over me now," I laughed,"—of proving it! But that doesn't matter. What Flora wants, of course, is to get rid of me."

My companion bravely concurred. "Never again to so much as look at you."

"So that what you've come to me now for," I asked, "is to speed me on my way?" Before she had time to reply, however, I had her in check. "I've a better idea—the result of my reflections. My going WOULD seem the right thing, and on Sunday I was terribly near it. Yet that won't do. It's YOU who must go. You must take Flora."

My visitor, at this, did speculate. "But where in the world—?"

"Away from here. Away from THEM. Away, even most of all, now, from me. Straight to her uncle."

"Only to tell on you—?"

"No, not 'only'! To leave me, in addition, with my remedy."

She was still vague. "And what IS your remedy?"

"Your loyalty, to begin with. And then Miles's."

She looked at me hard. "Do you think he—?"

"Won't, if he has the chance, turn on me? Yes, I venture still to think it. At all events, I want to try. Get off with his sister as soon as possible and leave me with him alone." I was amazed, myself, at the spirit I had still in reserve, and therefore perhaps a trifle the more disconcerted at the way in which, in spite of this fine example of it, she hesitated. "There's one thing, of course," I went on: "they mustn't, before she goes, see each other for three seconds." Then it came over me that, in spite of Flora's presumable sequestration from the instant of her return from the pool, it might already be too late. "Do you mean," I anxiously asked, "that they HAVE met?"

At this she quite flushed. "Ah, miss, I'm not such a fool as that! If I've been obliged to leave her three or four times, it has been each time with one of the maids, and at present, though she's alone, she's locked in safe. And yet—and yet!" There were too many things.

"And yet what?"

"Well, are you so sure of the little gentleman?"

"I'm not sure of anything but YOU. But I have, since last evening, a new hope. I think he wants to give me an opening. I do believe that—poor little exquisite wretch!—he wants to speak. Last evening, in the firelight and the silence, he sat with me for two hours as if it were just coming."

Mrs. Grose looked hard, through the window, at the gray, gathering day. "And did it come?"

"No, though I waited and waited, I confess it didn't, and it was without a breach of the silence or so much as a faint allusion to his sister's condition and absence that we at last kissed for good night. All the same," I continued, "I can't, if her uncle sees her, consent to his seeing her brother without my having given the boy—and most of all because things have got so bad—a little more time."

My friend appeared on this ground more reluctant than I could quite understand. "What do you mean by more time?"

"Well, a day or two—really to bring it out. He'll then be on MY side—of which you see the importance. If nothing comes, I shall only fail, and you will, at the worst, have helped me by doing, on your arrival in town, whatever you may have found possible." So I put it before her, but she continued for a little so inscrutably embarrassed that I came again to her aid. "Unless, indeed," I wound up, "you really want NOT to go."

I could see it, in her face, at last clear itself; she put out her hand to me as a pledge. "I'll go—I'll go. I'll go this morning."

I wanted to be very just. "If you SHOULD wish still to wait, I would engage she shouldn't see me."

"No, no: it's the place itself. She must leave it." She held me a moment with heavy eyes, then brought out the rest. "Your idea's the right one. I myself, miss—"

"Well?"

"I can't stay."

The look she gave me with it made me jump at possibilities. "You mean that, since yesterday, you HAVE seen—?"

She shook her head with dignity. "I've HEARD—!"

"Heard?"

"From that child—horrors! There!" she sighed with tragic relief. "On my honor, miss, she says things—!" But at this evocation she broke down; she dropped, with a sudden sob, upon my sofa and, as I had seen her do before, gave way to all the grief of it.

It was quite in another manner that I, for my part, let myself go. "Oh, thank God!"

She sprang up again at this, drying her eyes with a groan. "'Thank God'?"

"It so justifies me!"

"It does that, miss!"

## Analysis: This is a wonderful moment where Mrs Grose feels bullied and harried into saying that the governess is right about the ghosts. This admission enables her to remove Flora from the governess's company by taking him to her uncle.

## Discussion point: Do you think Flora really confessed to Mrs Grose about the ghosts?

I couldn't have desired more emphasis, but I just hesitated. "She's so horrible?"

I saw my colleague scarce knew how to put it. "Really shocking."

"And about me?"

"About you, miss—since you must have it. It's beyond everything, for a young lady; and I can't think wherever she must have picked up—"

"The appalling language she applied to me? I can, then!" I broke in with a laugh that was doubtless significant enough.

It only, in truth, left my friend still more grave. "Well, perhaps I ought to also—since I've heard some of it before! Yet I can't bear it," the poor woman went on while, with the same movement, she glanced, on my dressing table, at the face of my watch. "But I must go back."

I kept her, however. "Ah, if you can't bear it—!"

"How can I stop with her, you mean? Why, just FOR that: to get her away. Far from this," she pursued, "far from THEM-"

"She may be different? She may be free?" I seized her almost with joy. "Then, in spite of yesterday, you BELIEVE—"

"In such doings?" Her simple description of them required, in the light of her expression, to be carried no further, and she gave me the whole thing as she had never done. "I believe."

Yes, it was a joy, and we were still shoulder to shoulder: if I might continue sure of that I should care but little what else happened. My support in the presence of disaster would be the same as it had been in my early need of confidence, and if my friend would answer for my honesty, I would answer for all the rest. On the point of taking leave of her, nonetheless, I was to some extent embarrassed. "There's one thing, of course—it occurs to me—to remember. My letter, giving the alarm, will have reached town before you."

I now perceived still more how she had been beating about the bush and how weary at last it had made her. "Your letter won't have got there. Your letter never went."

"What then became of it?"

"Goodness knows! Master Miles—"

"Do you mean HE took it?" I gasped.

She hung fire, but she overcame her reluctance. "I mean that I saw yesterday, when I came back with Miss Flora, that it wasn't where you had put it. Later in the evening I had the chance to question Luke, and he declared that he had neither noticed nor touched it." We could only exchange, on this, one of our deeper mutual soundings, and it was Mrs. Grose who first brought up the plumb with an almost elated "You see!"

"Yes, I see that if Miles took it instead he probably will have read it and destroyed it."

"And don't you see anything else?"

I faced her a moment with a sad smile. "It strikes me that by this time your eyes are open even wider than mine."

They proved to be so indeed, but she could still blush, almost, to show it. "I make out now what he must have done at school." And she gave, in her simple sharpness, an almost droll disillusioned nod. "He stole!"

I turned it over—I tried to be more judicial. "Well—perhaps."

She looked as if she found me unexpectedly calm. "He stole LETTERS!"

She couldn't know my reasons for a calmness after all pretty shallow; so I showed them off as I might. "I hope then it was to more purpose than in this case! The note, at any rate, that I put on the table yesterday," I pursued, "will have given him so scant an advantage—for it contained only the bare demand for an interview—that he is already much ashamed of having gone so far for so little, and that what he had on his mind last evening was precisely the need of confession." I seemed to myself, for the instant, to have mastered it, to see it all. "Leave us, leave us"—I was already, at the door, hurrying her off. "I'll get it out of him. He'll meet me— he'll confess. If he confesses, he's saved. And if he's saved—"

"Then YOU are?" The dear woman kissed me on this, and I took her farewell. "I'll save you without him!" she cried as she went.

> **Analysis:** Now convinced that Miles intercepted her letter to the master, the governess determines to find out what she thinks is the truth. The crucial lines here are: 'I'll get it out of him. He'll meet me – he'll confess. If he confesses, he's saved. And if he's saved– ' What is important that the governess really believes that confession will lead to him being saved: her mission has taken upon a religious quality. She is like a priest exorcising someone. This is somewhat ironical because she has stated her religious beliefs very strongly.

> **Discussion point:** How does James build up the tension here? Would a confession save Miles? What would save him?

## Questions

Why does Mrs Grose wake the governess and what does she tell her?

What does the governess instruct Mrs Grose to do?

What does Mrs Grose say Flora has been saying about the governess?

How does the governess respond to these accusations?

What happened to the letter?

GCSE style question: how does James make the revelation about what Flora has been saying about the governess a shocking moment in the story?

GCSE style question: why do you think James never reveals to us what accusation Flora actually said to Mrs Grose about the governess?

A Level style question: compare and contrast the accusations in this story with another relevant text which contains accusations.

Creative response: write an account of Flora's accusations.

Creative response: write Mrs Grose's reflections on Flora's accusations in a diary entry.

Creative response: predict what might happen next.

You can find brief answers in the section, **Answers to the Questions**.

# Chapter 22

Yet it was when she had got off—and I missed her on the spot—that the great pinch really came. If I had counted on what it would give me to find myself alone with Miles, I speedily perceived, at least, that it would give me a measure. No hour of my stay in fact was so assailed with apprehensions as that of my coming down to learn that the carriage containing Mrs. Grose and my younger pupil had already rolled out of the gates. Now I WAS, I said to myself, face to face with the elements, and for much of the rest of the day, while I fought my weakness, I could consider that I had been supremely rash. It was a tighter place still than I had yet turned round in; all the more that, for the first time, I could see in the aspect of others a confused reflection of the crisis. What had happened naturally caused them all to stare; there was too little of the explained, throw out whatever we might, in the suddenness of my colleague's act. The maids and the men looked blank; the effect of which on my nerves was an aggravation until I saw the necessity of making it a positive aid. It was precisely, in short, by just clutching the helm that I avoided total wreck; and I dare say that, to bear up at all, I became, that morning, very grand and very dry. I welcomed the consciousness that I was charged with much to do, and I caused it to be known as well that, left thus to myself, I was quite remarkably firm. I wandered with that manner, for the next hour or two, all over the place and looked, I have no doubt, as if I were ready for any onset. So, for the benefit of whom it might concern, I paraded with a sick heart.

The person it appeared least to concern proved to be, till dinner, little Miles himself. My perambulations had given me, meanwhile, no glimpse of him, but they had tended to make more public the change taking place in our relation as a consequence of his having at the piano, the day before, kept me, in Flora's interest, so beguiled and befooled. The stamp of publicity had of course been fully given by her confinement and departure, and the change itself was now ushered in by our nonobservance of the regular custom of the schoolroom. He had already disappeared when, on my way down, I pushed open his door, and I learned below that he had breakfasted—in the presence of a couple of the maids—with Mrs. Grose and his sister. He had then gone out, as he said, for a stroll; than which nothing, I reflected, could better have expressed his frank view of the abrupt transformation of my office. What he would not permit this office to consist of was yet to be settled; there was a queer relief, at all events—I mean for myself in especial—in the renouncement of one pretension. If so much had sprung to the surface, I scarce put it too strongly in saying that what perhaps sprung highest was the absurdity of our prolonging the fiction that I had anything more to teach him. It sufficiently stuck out that, by tacit little tricks in which even more than myself he carried out the care for my dignity, I had had to appeal to him to let me off straining to meet him on the ground of his true capacity. He had at any rate his freedom now; I was never to touch it again; as I had amply shown, moreover, when, on his joining me in the schoolroom the previous night, I had uttered, on the subject of the interval just concluded, neither challenge nor hint. I had too much, from this moment, my other ideas. Yet when he at last arrived, the difficulty of applying them, the accumulations of my problem, were brought straight home to me by the beautiful little presence on which what had occurred had as yet, for the eye, dropped neither stain nor shadow.

To mark, for the house, the high state I cultivated I decreed that my meals with the boy should be served, as we called it, downstairs; so that I had been awaiting him in the ponderous pomp of the room outside of the window of which I had had from Mrs. Grose, that first scared Sunday, my flash of something it would scarce have done to call light. Here at present I felt afresh—for I had felt it again and again—how my equilibrium depended on the success of my rigid will, the will to shut my eyes as tight as possible to the truth that what I had to deal with was, revoltingly, against nature. I could only get on at all by taking "nature" into my confidence and my account, by treating my monstrous ordeal as a push in a direction unusual, of course, and unpleasant, but demanding, after all, for a fair front, only another turn of the screw of ordinary human virtue. No attempt, nonetheless, could well require more tact than just this attempt to supply, one's self, ALL the nature. How could I put even a little of that article into a suppression of reference to what had occurred? How, on the other hand, could I make reference without a new plunge into the hideous obscure? Well, a sort of answer, after a time, had come to me, and it was so far confirmed as that I was met, incontestably, by the quickened vision of what was rare in my little companion. It was indeed as if he had found even now—as he had so often found at lessons—still some other delicate way to ease me off. Wasn't there light in the fact which, as we shared our solitude, broke out with a specious glitter it had never yet quite worn?—the fact that (opportunity aiding, precious opportunity which had now come) it would be preposterous, with a child so endowed, to forego the help one might wrest from absolute intelligence? What had his intelligence been given him for but to save him? Mightn't one, to reach his mind, risk the stretch of an angular arm over his character? It was as if, when we were face to face in the dining room, he had literally shown me the way. The roast mutton was on the table, and I had dispensed with attendance. Miles, before he sat down, stood a moment with his hands in his pockets and looked at the joint, on which he seemed on the point of passing some humorous judgment. But what he presently produced was: "I say, my dear, is she really very awfully ill?"

"Little Flora? Not so bad but that she'll presently be better. London will set her up. Bly had ceased to agree with her. Come here and take your mutton."

He alertly obeyed me, carried the plate carefully to his seat, and, when he was established, went on. "Did Bly disagree with her so terribly suddenly?"

"Not so suddenly as you might think. One had seen it coming on."

"Then why didn't you get her off before?"

"Before what?"

"Before she became too ill to travel."

I found myself prompt. "She's NOT too ill to travel: she only might have become so if she had stayed. This was just the moment to seize. The journey will dissipate the influence"—oh, I was grand!—"and carry it off."

"I see, I see"—Miles, for that matter, was grand, too. He settled to his repast with the charming little "table manner" that, from the day of his arrival, had relieved me of all grossness of admonition. Whatever he had been driven from school for, it was not for ugly feeding. He was irreproachable, as always, today; but he was unmistakably more conscious.

He was discernibly trying to take for granted more things than he found, without assistance, quite easy; and he dropped into peaceful silence while he felt his situation. Our meal was of the briefest—mine a vain pretense, and I had the things immediately removed. While this was done Miles stood again with his hands in his little pockets and his back to me—stood and looked out of the wide window through which, that other day, I had seen what pulled me up. We continued silent while the maid was with us—as silent, it whimsically occurred to me, as some young couple who, on their wedding journey, at the inn, feel shy in the presence of the waiter. He turned round only when the waiter had left us. "Well—so we're alone!"

## Questions

Once Mrs Grose and Flora have gone, what does the governess focus upon?

What does Miles ask about at dinner?

What does the governess tell him?

What does Miles say when the waiter leaves?

GCSE style question: how does James generate suspense with the conversation at dinner?

A Level style question: compare and contrast descriptions of dinner in this story and another text of your choice.

Creative response: write Miles's diary for this chapter.

Creative response: predict what will happen next.

You can find brief answers in the section, **Answers to the Questions**.

# Chapter 23

"Oh, more or less." I fancy my smile was pale. "Not absolutely. We shouldn't like that!" I went on.

"No—I suppose we shouldn't. Of course we have the others."

"We have the others—we have indeed the others," I concurred.

"Yet even though we have them," he returned, still with his hands in his pockets and planted there in front of me, "they don't much count, do they?"

I made the best of it, but I felt wan. "It depends on what you call 'much'!"

"Yes"—with all accommodation—"everything depends!" On this, however, he faced to the window again and presently reached it with his vague, restless, cogitating step. He remained there awhile, with his forehead against the glass, in contemplation of the stupid shrubs I knew and the dull things of November. I had always my hypocrisy of "work," behind which, now, I gained the sofa. Steadying myself with it there as I had repeatedly done at those moments of torment that I have described as the moments of my knowing the children to be given to something from which I was barred, I sufficiently obeyed my habit of being prepared for the worst. But an extraordinary impression dropped on me as I extracted a meaning from the boy's embarrassed back—none other than the impression that I was not barred now. This inference grew in a few minutes to sharp intensity and seemed bound up with the direct perception that it was positively HE who was. The frames and squares of the great window were a kind of image, for him, of a kind of failure. I felt that I saw him, at any rate, shut in or shut out. He was admirable, but not comfortable: I took it in with a throb of hope. Wasn't he looking, through the haunted pane, for something he couldn't see?—and wasn't it the first time in the whole business that he had known such a lapse? The first, the very first: I found it a splendid portent. It made him anxious, though he watched himself; he had been anxious all day and, even while in his usual sweet little manner he sat at table, had needed all his small strange genius to give it a gloss. When he at last turned round to meet me, it was almost as if this genius had succumbed. "Well, I think I'm glad Bly agrees with ME!"

"You would certainly seem to have seen, these twenty-four hours, a good deal more of it than for some time before. I hope," I went on bravely, "that you've been enjoying yourself."

"Oh, yes, I've been ever so far; all round about—miles and miles away. I've never been so free."

He had really a manner of his own, and I could only try to keep up with him. "Well, do you like it?"

He stood there smiling; then at last he put into two words—"Do YOU?"—more discrimination than I had ever heard two words contain. Before I had time to deal with that, however, he continued as if with the sense that this was an impertinence to be softened. "Nothing could be more charming than the way you take it, for of course if we're alone together now it's you that are alone most. But I hope," he threw in, "you don't particularly mind!"

"Having to do with you?" I asked. "My dear child, how can I help minding? Though I've renounced all claim to your company—you're so beyond me—I at least greatly enjoy it. What else should I stay on for?"

He looked at me more directly, and the expression of his face, graver now, struck me as the most beautiful I had ever found in it. "You stay on just for THAT?"

"Certainly. I stay on as your friend and from the tremendous interest I take in you till something can be done for you that may be more worth your while. That needn't surprise you." My voice trembled so that I felt it impossible to suppress the shake. "Don't you remember how I told you, when I came and sat on your bed the night of the storm, that there was nothing in the world I wouldn't do for you?"

"Yes, yes!" He, on his side, more and more visibly nervous, had a tone to master; but he was so much more successful than I that, laughing out through his gravity, he could pretend we were pleasantly jesting. "Only that, I think, was to get me to do something for YOU!"

"It was partly to get you to do something," I conceded. "But, you know, you didn't do it."

"Oh, yes," he said with the brightest superficial eagerness, "you wanted me to tell you something."

"That's it. Out, straight out. What you have on your mind, you know."

"Ah, then, is THAT what you've stayed over for?"

**Analysis:** There is an unhinged quality to the conversation here. The governess admits that she has renounced her position but wants to stay on as a friend. Suddenly, the governess seems to have renounced her role as an authority figure: she has "renounced all claim" to his company. She is purely there to be a friend, to save him from himself as it were. The tension is increased because the governess is now alone with Miles.

**Discussion point:** What do you think of Miles' answers? How does James present him here? As a victim or a tormentor?

He spoke with a gaiety through which I could still catch the finest little quiver of resentful passion; but I can't begin to express the effect upon me of an implication of surrender even so faint. It was as if what I had yearned for had come at last only to astonish me. "Well, yes—I may as well make a clean breast of it, it was precisely for that."

He waited so long that I supposed it for the purpose of repudiating the assumption on which my action had been founded; but what he finally said was: "Do you mean now—here?"

"There couldn't be a better place or time." He looked round him uneasily, and I had the rare—oh, the queer!—impression of the very first symptom I had seen in him of the approach of immediate fear. It was as if he were suddenly afraid of me—which struck me indeed as perhaps the best thing to make him. Yet in the very pang of the effort I felt it vain to try sternness, and I heard myself the next instant so gentle as to be almost grotesque. "You want so to go out again?"

"Awfully!" He smiled at me heroically, and the touching little bravery of it was enhanced by his actually flushing with pain. He had picked up his hat, which he had brought in, and stood twirling it in a way that gave me, even as I was just nearly reaching port, a perverse horror of what I was doing. To do it in ANY way was an act of violence, for what did it consist of but the obtrusion of the idea of grossness and guilt on a small helpless creature who had been for me a revelation of the possibilities of beautiful intercourse? Wasn't it base to create for a being so exquisite a mere alien awkwardness? I suppose I now read into our situation a clearness it couldn't have had at the time, for I seem to see our poor eyes already lighted with some spark of a prevision of the anguish that was to come. So we circled about, with terrors and scruples, like fighters not daring to close. But it was for each other we feared! That kept us a little longer suspended and unbruised. "I'll tell you everything," Miles said—"I mean I'll tell you anything you like. You'll stay on with me, and we shall both be all right, and I WILL tell you—I WILL. But not now."

"Why not now?"

My insistence turned him from me and kept him once more at his window in a silence during which, between us, you might have heard a pin drop. Then he was before me again with the air of a person for whom, outside, someone who had frankly to be reckoned with was waiting. "I have to see Luke."

I had not yet reduced him to quite so vulgar a lie, and I felt proportionately ashamed. But, horrible as it was, his lies made up my truth. I achieved thoughtfully a few loops of my knitting. "Well, then, go to Luke, and I'll wait for what you promise. Only, in return for that, satisfy, before you leave me, one very much smaller request."

He looked as if he felt he had succeeded enough to be able still a little to bargain. "Very much smaller—?"

"Yes, a mere fraction of the whole. Tell me"—oh, my work preoccupied me, and I was offhand!—"if, yesterday afternoon, from the table in the hall, you took, you know, my letter."

**Analysis:** Here, the governess now seeks to find out the truth about the stealing of the letter. What is important to appreciate here is James' artistry in building up to this moment. The discovery of a relatively trivial misdemeanour has the weight of a truly momentous revelation: for the governess it proves he is in league with the ghosts.

**Discussion point:** Why does the letter become so significant in the novel?

## Questions

What does Miles say when the governess claims that they are not totally alone?

What does Miles say about Bly?

What does the governess say she misses?

What does Miles agree to do and when does he agree to do it?

What does the governess ask him about the letter?

GCSE style question: how does James's present Miles and the governess in this chapter? How does he generate suspense with his representation of these characters?

A Level style question: compare and contrast how revelations are presented in this story (the whole story) and another relevant text of your choice.

Creative response: write Miles's 'confession'.

You can find brief answers in the section, **Answers to the Questions**.

# Chapter 24

My sense of how he received this suffered for a minute from something that I can describe only as a fierce split of my attention—a stroke that at first, as I sprang straight up, reduced me to the mere blind movement of getting hold of him, drawing him close, and, while I just fell for support against the nearest piece of furniture, instinctively keeping him with his back to the window. The appearance was full upon us that I had already had to deal with here: Peter Quint had come into view like a sentinel before a prison. The next thing I saw was that, from outside, he had reached the window, and then I knew that, close to the glass and glaring in through it, he offered once more to the room his white face of damnation. It represents but grossly what took place within me at the sight to say that on the second my decision was made; yet I believe that no woman so overwhelmed ever in so short a time recovered her grasp of the ACT. It came to me in the very horror of the immediate presence that the act would be, seeing and facing what I saw and faced, to keep the boy himself unaware. The inspiration—I can call it by no other name—was that I felt how voluntarily, how transcendently, I MIGHT. It was like fighting with a demon for a human soul, and when I had fairly so appraised it I saw how the human soul—held out, in the tremor of my hands, at arm's length—had a perfect dew of sweat on a lovely childish forehead. The face that was close to mine was as white as the face against the glass, and out of it presently came a sound, not low nor weak, but as if from much further away, that I drank like a waft of fragrance.

"Yes—I took it."

At this, with a moan of joy, I enfolded, I drew him close; and while I held him to my breast, where I could feel in the sudden fever of his little body the tremendous pulse of his little heart, I kept my eyes on the thing at the window and saw it move and shift its posture. I have likened it to a sentinel, but its slow wheel, for a moment, was rather the prowl of a baffled beast. My present quickened courage, however, was such that, not too much to let it through, I had to shade, as it were, my flame. Meanwhile the glare of the face was again at the window, the scoundrel fixed as if to watch and wait. It was the very confidence that I might now defy him, as well as the positive certitude, by this time, of the child's unconsciousness, that made me go on. "What did you take it for?"

"To see what you said about me."

"You opened the letter?"

"I opened it."

My eyes were now, as I held him off a little again, on Miles's own face, in which the collapse of mockery showed me how complete was the ravage of uneasiness. What was prodigious was that at last, by my success, his sense was sealed and his communication stopped: he knew that he was in presence, but knew not of what, and knew still less that I also was and that I did know. And what did this strain of trouble matter when my eyes went back to the window only to see that the air was clear again and—by my personal triumph—the influence quenched? There was nothing there. I felt that the cause was mine and that I should surely get ALL. "And you found nothing!"—I let my elation out.

He gave the most mournful, thoughtful little headshake. "Nothing."

"Nothing, nothing!" I almost shouted in my joy.

"Nothing, nothing," he sadly repeated.

I kissed his forehead; it was drenched. "So what have you done with it?"

"I've burned it."

"Burned it?" It was now or never. "Is that what you did at school?"
Oh, what this brought up! "At school?"

## Analysis: There is a terrible poignancy here; Miles simply wanted to know what was being said about him. In such a way, James reveals how the written word has a huge power and grip upon the imaginations of the children: they want to know what is being reported about them. Miles is especially keen to know how he is presented to his uncle, who he views as a surrogate father. The governess's descriptions of Miles are very significant. In particular, we realise there is an important turning point when she says: "the collapse of mockery showed me how complete was the ravage of uneasiness". The cheeky expression which he had hitherto been presenting to the governess has "collapsed" indicating that this is a traumatic event. He is now ravaged by "uneasiness", in other words he is being destroyed by it. Most strikingly, now that he has confessed the ghostly face of Quint has now disappeared at the window: "the air was clear again" and "the influence quenched". The governess feels she has defeated the ghosts by extracting the truth from Miles.

## Discussion point: Why is Miles drenched in sweat? Why is he ravaged by uneasiness do you think?

"Did you take letters?—or other things?"
"Other things?" He appeared now to be thinking of something far off and that reached him only through the pressure of his anxiety. Yet it did reach him. "Did I STEAL?"
I felt myself redden to the roots of my hair as well as wonder if it were more strange to put to a gentleman such a question or to see him take it with allowances that gave the very distance of his fall in the world. "Was it for that you mightn't go back?"
The only thing he felt was rather a dreary little surprise. "Did you know I mightn't go back?"
"I know everything."
He gave me at this the longest and strangest look. "Everything?"
"Everything. Therefore DID you—?" But I couldn't say it again.
Miles could, very simply. "No. I didn't steal."
My face must have shown him I believed him utterly; yet my hands—but it was for pure tenderness—shook him as if to ask him why, if it was all for nothing, he had condemned me to months of torment. "What then did you do?"
He looked in vague pain all round the top of the room and drew his breath, two or three times over, as if with difficulty. He might have been standing at the bottom of the sea and raising his eyes to some faint green twilight. "Well—I said things."
"Only that?"
"They thought it was enough!"
"To turn you out for?"
Never, truly, had a person "turned out" shown so little to explain it as this

little person! He appeared to weigh my question, but in a manner quite detached and almost helpless. "Well, I suppose I oughtn't."

"But to whom did you say them?"

He evidently tried to remember, but it dropped—he had lost it. "I don't know!"

He almost smiled at me in the desolation of his surrender, which was indeed practically, by this time, so complete that I ought to have left it there. But I was infatuated—I was blind with victory, though even then the very effect that was to have brought him so much nearer was already that of added separation. "Was it to everyone?" I asked.

"No; it was only to—" But he gave a sick little headshake. "I don't remember their names."

"Were they then so many?"

"No—only a few. Those I liked."

Those he liked? I seemed to float not into clearness, but into a darker obscure, and within a minute there had come to me out of my very pity the appalling alarm of his being perhaps innocent. It was for the instant confounding and bottomless, for if he WERE innocent, what then on earth was I? Paralyzed, while it lasted, by the mere brush of the question, I let him go a little, so that, with a deep-drawn sigh, he turned away from me again; which, as he faced toward the clear window, I suffered, feeling that I had nothing now there to keep him from. "And did they repeat what you said?" I went on after a moment.

He was soon at some distance from me, still breathing hard and again with the air, though now without anger for it, of being confined against his will. Once more, as he had done before, he looked up at the dim day as if, of what had hitherto sustained him, nothing was left but an unspeakable anxiety. "Oh, yes," he nevertheless replied—"they must have repeated them. To those THEY liked," he added.

There was, somehow, less of it than I had expected; but I turned it over. "And these things came round—?"

"To the masters? Oh, yes!" he answered very simply. "But I didn't know they'd tell."

"The masters? They didn't—they've never told. That's why I ask you."

He turned to me again his little beautiful fevered face. "Yes, it was too bad."

"Too bad?"

"What I suppose I sometimes said. To write home."

I can't name the exquisite pathos of the contradiction given to such a speech by such a speaker; I only know that the next instant I heard myself throw off with homely force: "Stuff and nonsense!" But the next after that I must have sounded stern enough. "What WERE these things?"

My sternness was all for his judge, his executioner; yet it made him avert himself again, and that movement made ME, with a single bound and an irrepressible cry, spring straight upon him. For there again, against the glass, as if to blight his confession and stay his answer, was the hideous author of our woe—the white face of damnation.

# Analysis: Quint reappears when the governess feels that Miles is being less than forthcoming about the things he said at school. Quint is "the white face of damnation". Again, the religious imagery is important because it suggests that Quint's ghost is a form of damnation for the living. In the governess' view, he damns people because he won't let them tell the truth about his world.

# Discussion point: Why does Quint reappear again just when the governess felt that the ghosts had been vanquished?

I felt a sick swim at the drop of my victory and all the return of my battle, so that the wildness of my veritable leap only served as a great betrayal. I saw him, from the midst of my act, meet it with a divination, and on the perception that even now he only guessed, and that the window was still to his own eyes free, I let the impulse flame up to convert the climax of his dismay into the very proof of his liberation. "No more, no more, no more!" I shrieked, as I tried to press him against me, to my visitant.

"Is she HERE?" Miles panted as he caught with his sealed eyes the direction of my words. Then as his strange "she" staggered me and, with a gasp, I echoed it, "Miss Jessel, Miss Jessel!" he with a sudden fury gave me back.

I seized, stupefied, his supposition—some sequel to what we had done to Flora, but this made me only want to show him that it was better still than that. "It's not Miss Jessel! But it's at the window—straight before us. It's THERE—the coward horror, there for the last time!"

At this, after a second in which his head made the movement of a baffled dog's on a scent and then gave a frantic little shake for air and light, he was at me in a white rage, bewildered, glaring vainly over the place and missing wholly, though it now, to my sense, filled the room like the taste of poison, the wide, overwhelming presence. "It's HE?"

I was so determined to have all my proof that I flashed into ice to challenge him. "Whom do you mean by 'he'?"

"Peter Quint—you devil!" His face gave again, round the room, its convulsed supplication. "WHERE?"

They are in my ears still, his supreme surrender of the name and his tribute to my devotion. "What does he matter now, my own?—what will he EVER matter? I have you," I launched at the beast, "but he has lost you forever!" Then, for the demonstration of my work, "There, THERE!" I said to Miles.

But he had already jerked straight round, stared, glared again, and seen but the quiet day. With the stroke of the loss I was so proud of he uttered the cry of a creature hurled over an abyss, and the grasp with which I recovered him might have been that of catching him in his fall. I caught him, yes, I held him—it may be imagined with what a passion; but at the end of a minute I began to feel what it truly was that I held. We were alone with the quiet day, and his little heart, dispossessed, had stopped.

Analysis: The brilliantly tense ending of the novel terminates with Miles' death. The scene is very ambiguous because we never quite sure whether it is the governess who has tormented, harried and terrified Miles to death with her talk of the ghosts, or whether the ghosts have claimed Miles for one of their own. Miles becomes furious with the governess; we are never quite sure why. The governess feels that she combating Quint, claiming that she has Miles, but that Quint has lost Miles forever. In the light of Miles' death, this is hugely and tragically ironic.

Discussion point: What was the cause of Miles' death? Why does James present Miles' death in such an ambiguous fashion?

## Questions

What is the governess distracted by during the conversation?
What does the governess do?
What does Miles confess about the letter?
What does the governess confront Miles about?
What does Miles say happened to him at school?
Who does Miles name and what does he call this person?
What does the governess point out and yell at?
What does Miles do?
GCSE style question: how does James make this such a thrilling and horrifying end to the novel?
A Level style question: compare and contrast the ending of this story with the ending of another relevant text of your choice.
Creative response: write what happens to the governess after this story during the rest of her life.
Creative response: write Peter Quint's observations of what happened.
You can find brief answers in the section, **Answers to the Questions**.

# Answers to the questions

IMPORTANT NOTE: the answers to these questions are deliberately very brief; many of them could be much longer, particularly the answers to the GCSE/ A Level/Creative Response questions which require argumentative, evaluative and personal responses as well as creative thought. Most of the time, I have not provided responses to GCSE/A Level/Creative sets of questions or repeated the questions again. It is best that you get peer or teacher feedback on those questions.

## Prologue

What do the guests at the house party think makes a creepy story? A ghost visiting a child.

What story does Douglas say he knows about? When a ghost visits two children.

What does Douglas need to do in order to tell the story? To send his servant to London to fetch the manuscript in which the story is told.

What connection does Douglas have with the author of the story? She was his sister's governess, with whom he was in love.

What does Douglas explain was the circumstances of the writing of the story? How old was the governess and why was she put in charge of two children? She was 20 years old, and was asked by a handsome uncle to look after his orphaned nephew and niece who live in a remote house in the country.

On what condition must the governess take the work? That she must never trouble the uncle with any problems.

Why does the governess possibly accept the position? Because she is attracted to the uncle.

## Chapter 1

Where is the country house? In Bly, a remote country house in Essex, England.

What is Flora like: how old, appearance, manners, and mood? She is the younger sister, she is very polite, but the governess does think she hears her crying behind closed doors in the house.

What does Mrs Grose say about Flora's brother? That he is good looking.

What does the governess do with Flora the next day? Flora shows her around the house.

What did the governess then feel about Bly, and what does she feel now? She felt very optimistic, but now feels Bly is ugly.

## Chapter 2

What is enclosed in the uncle's letter to the governess which troubles her? A letter from Miles's headmaster saying he is no longer welcome at the school.

What is Mrs Grose's response to the news about Miles and the school? She doesn't understand why Miles was expelled.

What does Mrs Grose say about Miles's behavior when the governess questions her again? She had known him to be bad, but this was to be expected from a boy.

What does Mrs Grose say about the previous governess who died? That she was young and pretty, but she avoids talking about her death.

## Chapter 3

What does the governess feel about Miles when she sees him and why? She feels he must be incapable of doing wrong because he is as beautiful and pure as Flora.

What does she decide to do about Miles's expulsion? Nothing.

What is the behavior of the children like? Very good.

What does the governess see when she goes for a walk one evening? A man standing on top of one of the house's towers who is looking at her.

What do you think Miles did wrong at school? Some critics suggest he spread rumours about other children, others that he was guilty of a sexual misdemeanor.

## Chapter 4

Why does the governess think Miles was expelled from the school? That he was too good for the "horrid, unclean world".

What troubles the governess about the children? That they seem impersonal, without any history to them.

What does the governess see at the window one Sunday? The man who she saw on the tower.

What does the governess do? She runs after him outside and finds that he has vanished.

What startles Mrs Grose? That the governess is suddenly outside, staring at her through the window.

## Chapter 5

What does the governess confess to Mrs Grose? That she saw a man at the window, and on the tower.

Why does the governess feel she can't go to church? That she must stay and protect the house from the intruder.

What does the governess say the intruder looked like after being questioned by Mrs Grose? That he was pale, with red hair and without a hat.

What does Mrs Grose say this person is like? Peter Quint, the former valet who was in charge until he died last year.

## Chapter 6

What does the governess suddenly realise about Quint as she discusses things with Mrs Grose? That he was looking for Miles.

What does the governess wonder about Miles? That he never mentioned Quint.

What does Mrs Grose say Quint's behavior was like with Miles? That he was too "free".

What does the governess come to see her role has to be at the house? That she has to protect the children.

What does the governess think she sees as she observes Flora playing by the bank of the lake? A third presence.

Where is Miles at this time? Inside.

## Chapter 7

What does the governess tell Mrs Grose about Flora and Miles? That the children know about the visitors; that Flora saw the lady the governess observed but said nothing.

What does the governess say the ghost looked like? That she was a woman, dressed in black, and that she appeared out of nowhere.

Who does the governess think this woman is? Miss Jessel, the former governess.

How does Mrs Grose defend Flora? She says she was innocent.

What does Mrs Grose say about Miss Jessel? That she was "infamous" and had an inappropriate relationship with Jessel.

What does the governess lament about? That the children are out of her control.

## Chapter 8

What does the governess feel when she returns to the children? Ashamed that she could have thought that Flora was cunning.

Why does the governess interrogate Mrs Grose? To find out how Miles was bad.

What does Mrs Grose tell the governess about Miles's misbehavior? That it only happened when he was with Quint.

Who was Flora with when Miles was with Quint? Miss Jessel.

How does Mrs Grose try to defend Miles? That he was not to blame for his bad behavior, but Quint was.

## Chapter 9

How does the governess's relationship with the children progress? It is very positive and affectionate.

Why does the governess think the children are possibly being nice? To hide something.

What happens one night when the governess is startled while reading? What does she do and see? She goes to the top of the stairway, her candle is blown out, and she sees Quint ascending half way up the stairs.

What does the governess do when she sees Quint? She stares at him, refusing to back down.

## Chapter 10

Where does the governess find Flora and why does it trouble her? She finds her behind a window blind and not in her bed. Flora has drawn the bed curtains, as if to deceive the governess that she is asleep in bed. The governess thinks Flora is looking outside.

Why does the governess find it difficult to sleep after this incident? She is worried about the ghosts, and the children. She has had a vision of Miss Jessel with her head in her hands at the bottom of the stairs which has disturbed her.

What happens when the governess finally decides to go to bed at the normal time? She wakes at midnight to find her candle has gone out.

Where does she find the children? What does she think Flora is doing? Flora is at the window and Miles is out on the lawn. She thinks Flora is communicating with Miss Jessel.

## Chapter 11

What does the governess tell Mrs Grose the next morning? That she had gone down to Miles on the lawn and he had followed her inside without speaking. He said that he had done it so that she would think him capable of being bad. He and Flora had deliberately planned this so that they would wake up the governess and she would investigate.

How does the governess respond to Miles's story about being bad? She embraces him.

## Chapter 12

What does the governess tell Mrs Grose about what she really thinks the children are up to? She thinks they are in league with Quint and Miss Jessel, and they are empty because their lives belong to the spirits.

What does the governess think Quint and Miss Jessel are planning? They want to destroy the children.

What are Mrs Grose's suggestions? That they should either go to their employer or ask him to come to them.

What is the governess's response? She threatens to leave if Mrs Grose tells their employer because he will be amused that her loneliness has driven her to this.

## Chapter 13

What does the governess think the children know? What is her evidence for this? They know that the governess knows about the ghosts. Her evidence is that they avoid talking about any topic that might relate to Quint and Miss Jessel.

As time passes, what does the governess think the children might be doing? That they are communicating with ghosts in her presence.

Why does the governess shut herself away? She feels unable to talk to the children about the ghosts; she doesn't know what to do; she tries to rehearse talking to them about the topic in her room.

What do the children ask her about? Why their uncle has not contacted them.

What does the governess suggest they do? Write letters to their uncle for educational purposes.

## Chapter 14

What does Miles ask the governess as they are going to church? When he will be going back to school.

Why does Miles want to go back to school? To be amongst his own sort.

What is the governess's response? That he is amongst his own sort with Flora.

What does the governess tell Miles about their uncle? That he doesn't care for Miles or Flora.

What does Miles say he will make his uncle do? Come to Bly.

## Chapter 15

What shocks the governess about Miles? That he is fully aware of his situation and has a plan to defy her.

What does the governess decide to do? Leave Bly.

Why does the governess change her mind? She sees Miss Jessel when she returns to the house in the school room and calls her a terrible, miserable woman.

## Chapter 16

What does Mrs Grose tell the governess the children have said when they get back from church? That they should do their best to please the governess, and not mention topics which upset her.

What does the governess say happened with her and Miss Jessel? That Miss Jessel had spoken to her about the torments of the dead and that she wants Flora.

What does the governess say which pleases Mrs Grose? That she will call for the children's uncle.

What does the governess now think was the reason for Miles's expulsion from school? Wickedness.

Why is the governess reluctant to write to the uncle? He will not believe her.

What is finally agreed and why? That the governess will write to the uncle because Mrs Grose breaks down in tears, and says she will write if the governess does not.

## Chapter 17

Why does the governess stop writing the letter? She gets up to listen at Miles's door and he calls her in.

What is Miles bothered about? The odd way that the governess is bringing him up.

What reason does the governess give for not sending Miles back to school? He'd never brought it up before.

Why does the governess embrace and kiss Miles? Because he speaks with such calm about wanting a change of environment and because she wants to learn more about why he was expelled from school.

Why does Miles shriek? Because there is a sudden gust in the room and the light goes out.

## Chapter 18

What does Mrs Grose ask the governess about and why is her answer not the whole truth? Mrs Grose asks about whether the governess has written the letter; the governess replies she has written it but doesn't say she hasn't sent it.

What does Miles ask for which pleases the governess? For her to play the piano.

What does the governess realise as she is playing the piano? That Flora is missing.

What does the governess think Miles is doing? Distracting her so that he can see Quint in the school room.

## Chapter 19

Where do the governess and Mrs Grose head to and why? To the lake, where Flora has gone to see Miss Jessel.

Where do they find Flora? Near the lake.

What does Flora appear to be puzzled about? She wonders where Mrs Grose and the governess's things are – their hats – and where Miles is.

What does governess say Flora must do? Tell her where Miss Jessel is.

## Chapter 20

Where does the governess see Miss Jessel? On the opposite bank.

What does Mrs Grose see? Nothing.

What does Flora insist Mrs Grose does? Take the governess away from her.

What does the governess think has happened to Flora? That Miss Jessel is speaking through Flora.

What does the governess notice about the position of the boat and why is this significant? That the boat is in its normal position, but had previously been near Flora.

GCSE style question: how does James make the confrontation with Flora a climatic moment in the story?

A Level style question: compare and contrast the climax in this novel with another climatic moment in a relevant text of your choice.

## Chapter 21

Why does Mrs Grose wake the governess and what does she tell her? That Flora is sick and terrified of the governess.

What does the governess instruct Mrs Grose to do? To take Flora to her uncle, but that Flora must not talk to Miles.

What does Mrs Grose say Flora has been saying about the governess? Really shocking things.

How does the governess respond to these accusations? That Flora picked up this language from Miss Jessel; that it proves she was right that Miss Jessel has corrupted Flora.

What happened to the letter? Miles took it and it wasn't sent.

## Chapter 22

Once Mrs Grose and Flora have gone, what does the governess focus upon? How she is going to confront Miles.

What does Miles ask about at dinner? His sister's illness.

What does the governess tell him? That Flora wasn't too ill to travel.

What does Miles say when the waiter leaves? That they are alone.

## Chapter 23

What does Miles say when the governess claims that they are not totally alone? That there are "the others".

What does Miles say about Bly? That it agrees with him.

What does the governess say she misses? Miles's company.

What does Miles agree to do when? To tell the governess everything but not now. He needs to see the servant Luke first.

What does the governess ask him about the letter? Whether he took it or not.

## Chapter 24

What is the governess distracted by during the conversation? Peter Quint looking in through the window.

What does the governess do? Makes sure Miles can't see the ghost by drawing him close and comforting him.

What does Miles confess about the letter? That he took it, read it to see what it said about him, and then seeing it said nothing, burnt it.

What does the governess confront Miles about? What he did at school to get expelled.

What does Miles say happened to him at school? That he "said things" to boys he liked.

Who does Miles name and what does he call this person? Peter Quint, who he calls a devil.

What does the governess point out and yell at? Peter Quint.

What does Miles do? He dies.

# Speaking and Listening Exercises

Work in a group and devise a **chatshow** based on the novel. Make sure that you have an interviewer (chat-show host) who questions the main characters in the novel about their thoughts and feelings regarding what has happened to them. The aim is that students need to show that they understand the storyline and characters by talking in role about the events in the novel. You can include dead characters such as Miles, Peter Quint and Miss Jessel.

You could put the governess on **trial**, accused of causing the death of Miles. Set things up so that you have a prosecuting lawyer who is accusing the governess of the crimes of child abuse, neglect and bullying. Have a defence lawyer who argues that there is evidence that both of these defendants should be treated leniently. Call witnesses for the prosecution and defence who are characters from the novel such as the uncle, Mrs Grose and Flora; or the author; or "made-up" characters such as a psychiatrist who has assessed the governess, school teachers from Miles's school, and his friends there etc. Use the trial to explore different views on the novel. Then possibly write it up as a script or review what you have learnt from doing it.

Put the main characters in **therapy:** the governess, Mrs Grose, Flora, Miles, and the uncle. Have them visit a therapist to discuss their problems with him/her. You could do this so that they go into therapy at various stages during the story, i.e. the governess when she first arrives, Mrs Grose talking about the children/governess/Quint/Jessel at the beginning, middle and end of the story; Miles and Flora at the different stages of the story. Write a review of what you have learnt from doing this afterwards.

Work in a group and devise a **radio drama** of the major parts of the novel. Different groups could work on different sections of the book; e.g. the governess's arrival, her first sightings of Quint, her growing horror about the children, her confrontation with Flora at the lake, and the death of Miles. Make the drama short and punchy. This exercise will help you get to know the text in much more depth: the editing of the novel will help you summarise key points.

# How to write top grade essays on the novel

In order to write a good essay about *The Turn of the Screw*, you need to understand it. You will need to know what the difficult vocabulary means and be aware of how the text is the product of the world it comes from: late nineteenth century England. You will also need to be aware of what the examiners for your particular question are looking for. For GCSE, it appears that most questions are, at the time of writing this guide, "extract based"; you will be given a small extract and asked to consider how the author builds suspense or drama in the extract, or presents the characters or key themes in a particular way. In order to achieve highly, you will need to answer the question carefully and not simply re-tell the extract; this is something that I have seen many good students do. The A Level questions are much more like the ones posed in the **essay question section** of this study guide and the A Level style questions posed at the end of the chapter questions. Sometimes, you might be asked to compare the novel with other literary texts, depending upon the nature of the task and/or exam board. For A Level, you need to be aware of other literary critics' views on the novel.

You should consider a few key questions:

For extract questions, consider how has the author **built up** to this particular moment? Think carefully about what the reader already knows before they have read the extract. You will need to know the story well in order to do this.

What literary devices does the author use to make the passage interesting or to reveal a particular character in a certain light? Think very carefully about the author's use of language: James's use of descriptions to create a certain atmosphere or paint a sketch of a character/event; his use of dialogue to reveal character and create drama/tension; his use of imagery (metaphors/similes/personification). You will need to pack your essay full of the relevant terminology if you want to aim for higher marks as it appears many mark schemes as a key requirement.

You need to be aware of a number of different interpretations of the novel. The weblinks below should help you with this.

Finally, you need to provide evidence and analysis to back up your points. As a cornerstone of your essay writing technique, you should be aware of the **PEEL** method of analysing texts: making a Point, providing Evidence, Explaining how your evidence endorses your point, and Linking to a new point.

# Writing about the story/narrative

I would strongly advise you to read my section on the **structure and themes of the novel here** before writing about the effects the narrative structure of the book creates. There are many, many things to say about the story of the book, but you should think about your own personal response as well: what did you find the most engaging parts of the novel and why? Look back over the notes you have made while you read the novel and use them to shape an original response. You need to avoid just re-telling the story, which is very easy to do in highly pressurised situations and you're not thinking straight!

# Writing about the characterisations

There are many websites which can help you with writing about the characters in the novel, already listed earlier on in this book. What most of them don't say is a very important thing I've already mentioned; James's characters are *not* real people, they are literary creations and we become interested in them because of their similarities and differences. A central technique of James's is to make the reader think about how and why characters are similar and different; we are constantly being invited to compare and contrast characters in our minds. This is a central way that James generates suspense and drama in the novel; the novel is full striking comparisons and contrasts. Where governess is passionate, impulsive, and powerful and the other characters at Bly are cautious, quiet and lacking in power. James reveals the children, Flora and Miles to be similar and different: Miles is labelled as naughty by Mrs Grose and his school, but Flora seems more cunning and just as scheming. Or not? We never quite know what the children are planning; are they in contact with the ghosts or is their supposed communication with Quint and Jessel just a figment of the governess's imagination? It is the ambivalence of the characters – never quite knowing whether they are telling the truth or not – which creates much of the suspense in the novel.

### Task

Look at some character studies online and devise a chart or **visual organiser** which illustrates the similarities and differences between the major characters, exploring the effects that these similarities and differences have upon the reader.

# Writing about the settings

Henry James is an interesting writer because he avoids describing the physical surroundings in depth; instead we gain more of a sense of the place from vividly drawn details and through the dialogue of the characters. Nevertheless, certain settings play a very important part in the book: the sighting of Quint on the tower, the school room, the lake and its surroundings, the bedrooms, windows etc. His technique is to briefly sketch what they might look like and then explore the governess's thoughts and feelings about being in that place. She rarely lingers long to describe what is actually there; it is her psychological state which is much more important. This, I think, gives the novel its ghostly, unreal quality.

You can find more information about settings here:

### Task

Look carefully at the use of settings in the novel; what purpose do they serve? Why does James set particular scenes in particular settings such as the school room, by the lake, on the stairs and in the bedrooms? Think also about the time of day/night he sets his scenes; how does the time of day create certain effects?

# Suspicion

A central technique of James is to make the reader feel suspicious about the characters' motives and actions. Once you begin to appreciate the role of suspicion in the novel and understand how James generates suspense from the governess's suspicion, you will be able to analyse how he makes the narrative dramatic. The central point is that we never quite know whether the governess's suspicions will be proven or whether she is right to be suspicious in the first place. Is the story the product of a paranoid mind, or is she right? Are the children in communication with Miss Jessel and Quint?

### Task

Look back over the novel, and work out when and where the governess is suspicious and what clues both back up her suspicions and undermine them. Devise a visual organiser which charts the suspicious moments so that you can see clearly on one page where such moments occur, and think about the effect they have upon the reader.

# Use of language

Above all, you need to analyse the effects of James's language upon the reader; exploring what the language makes the reader think, feel and see.

### Task

Devise a chart/visual organiser/notes on the different types of language James uses in the novel, providing quotes and examples for the following types of language:

Descriptive language: language which describes people, places and situations

Imagery: language which makes comparisons

Important dialogue: important quotes that people say that make the plot move on.

## Useful links

These websites contain some incisive analysis on the use of language.

**http://www.shmoop.com/turn-of-the-screw/writing-style.html**
**http://www.sparknotes.com/lit/screw/themes.html**

**http://www.literary-articles.com/2010/02/narrative-technique-of-turn-of-screw.html**
**http://www.cummingsstudyguides.net/Guides4/TurnScrew.html**
**http://www.ocr.org.uk/Images/80971-unit-f661-the-turn-of-the-screw-english-reading-list.pdf**

# Possible essay titles

To what extent is *The Turn of the Screw* a ghost story?

'The children in the novel deserve our pity more than our condemnation.' To what extent do you agree with this statement?

To what extent is *The Turn of the Screw* a novel about oppression?

What role does social class play in the novel?

How and why do the settings play such an important role in the novel?

Analyse and explore the role dialogue plays in the novel.

# Glossary

**Anonymous** – not given a name, without a name

**Apparition** – ghost

**Controlling** – trying to control someone in an inappropriate way

**Correspondent** – a journalist

**Corruption** – lack of integrity or honesty (especially susceptibility to bribery); use of a position of trust for dishonest gain; being immoral, deliberately bad

**Damnation** -- the state of being condemned to eternal punishment in Hell

**Genre** – type of story, e.g. ghost story, Western etc

**Hallucination** – a vision, or illusory perception; a common symptom of severe mental disorder

**Hysteria** -- craze: state of violent mental agitation; excessive or uncontrollable fear; neurotic disorder characterized by violent emotional outbreaks and disturbances of sensory and motor functions

**Interrogates** – questions very closely

**Malign influence** – a bad or evil influence

**Morally depraved** – behaving in an evil and corrupt way

**Neurosis** -- any of various mental or emotional disorders, such as hypochondria or neurasthenia, arising from no apparent organic lesion or change and involving symptoms such as insecurity, anxiety, depression, and irrational fears, but without psychotic symptoms such as delusions or hallucinations

**Neurotic** – a person who has neurosis, a very anxious, mentally unstable person

**Paranoia** – extreme suspicion, a psychological disorder characterized by delusions of persecution or grandeur

**Poignant** – deeply moving; a state of deeply felt distress or sorrow; "a moment of extraordinary poignancy"

**Psychological** -- mental or emotional as opposed to physical in nature; "give psychological support"; "psychological warfare"

**Repressed** – holding back one's true feelings, burying feelings

**Resonance** – a moment of truth and perception

**Sacrosanct** -- holy

**Sexual licentiousness** – being sexually abandoned, behaving promiscuously

**Spiritual phenomena** – ghosts, spirits

**Veneer** – a cover, facade

**Unmitigated Disaster** – a total catastrophe

# About the Author

Francis Gilbert is a Lecturer in Education at Goldsmiths, University of London, teaching on the PGCE Secondary English programme and the MA in Children's Literature with Professor Michael Rosen. Previously, he worked for a quarter of a century in various English state schools teaching English and Media Studies to 11-18 year olds. He has also moonlighted as a journalist, novelist and social commentator both in the UK and international media. He is the author of *Teacher On The Run*, *Yob Nation*, *Parent Power*, *Working The System -- How To Get The Very Best State Education for Your Child*, and a novel about school, *The Last Day Of Term*. His first book, *I'm A Teacher, Get Me Out Of Here* was a big hit, becoming a bestseller and being serialised on Radio 4. In his role as an English teacher, he has taught many classic texts over the years and has developed a great many resources to assist readers with understanding, appreciating and responding to them both analytically and creatively. This led him to set up his own small publishing company FGI Publishing (fgipublishing.com) which has published his study guides as well as a number of books by other authors, including Roger Titcombe's *Learning Matters* and Tim Cadman's *The Changes*.

He is the co-founder, with Melissa Benn and Fiona Millar, of The Local Schools Network, **www.localschoolsnetwork.org.uk**, a blog that celebrates non-selective state schools, and also has his own website, **www.francisgilbert.co.uk** and a Mumsnet blog, **www.talesbehindtheclassroomdoor.co.uk**.

He has appeared numerous times on radio and TV, including Newsnight, the Today Programme, Woman's Hour and the Russell Brand Show. In June 2015, he was awarded a PhD in Creative Writing and Education by the University of London.

Printed in Great Britain
by Amazon

33445813R00080